Like a Garden
A Biblical Spirituality of Growth

Sara Covin Juengst

Westminster John Knox Press
Louisville, Kentucky

Scripture quotations from the New Revised Standard Version of the Bible are copyright © 1989 by the Division of Christian Education of the National Council of the Churches of Christ in the U.S.A. and are used by permission.

Book design by Jennifer K. Cox
Cover design by Fearless Designs
Cover and internal illustrations by Katherine Pinard

First edition

Published by Westminster John Knox Press
Louisville, Kentucky

This book is printed on acid-free paper that meets the American National Standards Institute Z39.48 standard. ⊗

PRINTED IN THE UNITED STATES OF AMERICA

96 97 98 99 00 01 02 03 04 05 — 10 9 8 7 6 5 4 3 2 1

Library of Congress Cataloging-in-Publication Data

Juengst, Sara Covin
     Like a garden : a biblical spirituality of growth / Sara Covin
Juengst.
          p.   cm.
     Includes bibliographical references.
     ISBN 0-664-25634-1 (alk. paper)
     1. Gardening in the Bible. 2. Gardening—Religious aspects—
Christianity.   I. Title.
BS680.G37J86   1996
248—dc20   95-46684

Like a Garden

This book is dedicated to Dan, who for four decades has provided the nurture, care, and support that has helped my garden grow.

CONTENTS

Foreword by Walter Brueggemann   ix

Preface   xi

1. Gardening in Biblical Times   1

2. The Garden of the Lord: Nourishment for Body and Soul   13

3. Connecting with Creation: Awareness and Responsibility   33

4. Like a Watered Garden: Healing and Renewal   47

5. Weeding and Pruning: Discipline and Confrontation   65

6. Bringing in the Sheaves: Hope and Thanksgiving   81

   Notes   99

FOREWORD

In this little book, Sara Juengst continues her rich and suggestive exploration of biblical imagery that lives close to life. Here soil and symbol meet. The "soil" reflects the actual garden dirt that Sara evidently has under her fingernails, garden dirt that informs her thinking and propels her imagination, garden dirt that invites, heals, and demands.

But this book on gardening is much more than a book on gardening. It is, at the same time, an act of vigorous theological imagination, in which Sara mobilizes her considerable learning, draws heavily on her rootage in Calvinism, and then springs beyond that rootage to a theology of creation not habituated in conventional Calvinism.

The outcome is a lively, engaging collage of images that are sure to set the reader off in new directions of imagination and faith. At the center stands God the Gardener, Juengst's dominant metaphor, who presides with care, planning, and discipline over the garden of the earth. From that central imagery arises a concern for ecology and the terrorizing of the garden now so broadly underway. That ethical concern is matched by a spirituality that focuses on discipline, task, and pruning.

But the symbol is never loosed from the soil. The faith on offer here is concrete, daily, palpable, and accessible. We are, all of us, pilgrims in a barren land. This book attends to the water that will make our deserts bloom.

Foreword

The book is a compelling practice of the permits of elasticity given in biblical rhetoric, in which the author moves freely toward symbolization but always back to the soil. Readers can anticipate a rich harvest.

WALTER BRUEGGEMANN
Columbia Theological Seminary

PREFACE

Some years ago, I wrote a poem that began, "It is a need I have to plant." The poem is lost, but the need remains. It surfaces anew each January when the seed catalogs arrive, it takes on urgency when spring warmth allows me to scatter seeds, and it finds deep satisfaction and a mysterious consolation when the first tiny, burgeoning green leaflets appear. I remember hearing a character in a television comedy express this aspect of spring fever in the words "If I don't get something to plant, I think I'll jump out of my skin."

I remember how proud my father was of his "Victory Garden" during World War II, although I was not exactly thrilled when he asked me to help hoe the weeds. I remember my mother, in her late seventies, picking her bountiful bean harvest with sweat running down her sun-reddened face. I've had garden plots in Africa, in the sandy soil of Florida, and in the red clay of Georgia and South Carolina. I read gardening books with relish and love to discuss composting and worm farming and nematodes with folk who know more than I do about those matters.

What is it about a garden that has such a strong attraction for those of us who no longer have to depend on our own harvests for daily sustenance? Why do so many otherwise sane people relish getting dirt under their fingernails and sweat on their brows? Why do we invest in seeds and plants and fertilizer, even when our gardens never turn out like the seed catalog pictures? Perhaps it is because garden-

Hope

xi

ing is a participation in hope, a symbol of our hunger to affirm the possibility and promise of new beginnings.

Throughout the Bible, the mystery of gardening is used again and again to illustrate a variety of themes: God's providential love and care, our connectedness to the earth and our responsibility for it, the necessity for spiritual growth and renewal, and the reality of our ultimate hope. The covenant itself was based on the understanding that we live in "the garden of the Lord," sustained by the Gardener who provides rain, sun, and land but who expects from us, in return, responsibility and commitment.

Because we live in a technological world, we are in danger of losing that sense of our connectedness to the land, as well as our recognition that "the earth is the Lord's and the fullness thereof." This book is for those who recognize that danger and would like to reclaim for themselves and for others that sense of connectedness by exploring biblical passages about gardens and gardening, about seedtime and harvest, about the joy of creation and the miracle of growth. It is also for pastors and educators and all who teach God's word and want a fresh understanding of such biblical metaphors as soil, seed, fruit, rain, plowing, planting, and harvesting. But above all, it is for gardeners: potted-plant gardeners, forty-acre gardeners, patio gardeners, weekend gardeners, and full-time gardeners—those devotees and dilettantes who know the joy of watching seeds grow and who "come home with shouts of joy, carrying their sheaves" (Ps. 126:6b).

Willington, South Carolina, 1995

1   GARDENING IN BIBLICAL TIMES

As long as the earth endures, seedtime and harvest . . . shall not cease.
—Genesis 8:22

Plant gardens and eat what they produce.
—Jeremiah 29:5

Anyone who tills the land will have plenty of bread,
    but one who follows worthless pursuits will have plenty of poverty.
—Proverbs 28:19

Oh, Adam was a gardener, and God who made him sees
That half a proper gardener's work is done upon his knees.
—Rudyard Kipling

To garden is to take part in mystery. To place seeds on the waiting earth, cover them with soil, moisten them, and wait in hope and expectation is a statement of faith. The people of the Bible understood this, so it is not surprising that Israel's poets and prophets made use of garden images in their proverbs and psalms, in allegories and parables, in blessings and prophetic utterances. Although the Bible is not a textbook on agriculture, few other ancient books give as much information about the agricultural life of the ancient Israelites as it does. Of the 2,600 types of plants found in Israel today, however, the Bible mentions only 110.[1] Genesis and Isaiah are the richest biblical sources of agricultural information, but nearly every other book in the Bible has at least one reference to gardening.

Gardening is one of the oldest human industries. It may have begun in the Near East as much as twelve thousand years ago. Cultivated grain seeds that date back nine thousand years have been discovered. The introduction of farming brought about significant changes in the lives of human beings. In fact, it is perhaps not too much to say that the discovery of gardening was the beginning of civilization as we know it.

As people settled down to farming after a nomadic life of hunting and gathering, their lives changed dramatically. For the first time, they began to live in permanent houses in towns and cities, and as a result, social structures and governments were formed. The need for gardening tools and equipment meant the development of technologies such as pottery and metalwork and stone carving. An economy based on agriculture led to commerce and trade as people exchanged the crops they had produced for goods they wanted and, later on, for money. Writing developed as a way to record these transactions.

Even religious life was influenced by agriculture. Harvest festivals became central to the worship of these agrarian folk. Moral laws were developed that centered on the use of agricultural resources to care for the poor through the sharing of food. These laws led to customs that we read about in the Old Testament, such as "gleaning," or leaving behind some of the wheat or grapes for the poor, who had no fields.

The Israelites experienced all these changes as they left their nomadic life to settle down in the land of Canaan. They became village dwellers instead of nomads. They divided the land into plots and began to learn how to sow and irrigate and prune and harvest the crops that would sustain them. But even as they began to develop their gardens, the basic premise underlying their activity was that the land really belonged to God. It is significant that many of the covenant laws were related to agriculture: to mundane matters such as crop rotation and cutting trees, to proper procedures for harvest festivals, and to the importance of sharing food with the less fortunate.

This golden thread—"the land belongs to God"—runs through the entire Old Testament, and it colored the way the people felt about the land. It is spelled out in Lev. 25:23: "The land shall not be sold in perpetuity, for the land is mine, with me you are but aliens and tenants." Respect and reverence for the land grew out of the covenant convictions that it was sacred, that it belonged to God, and that the Israelites were to be stewards of it. This belief formed the underlying motivation for the harvest festivals: the Feast of Weeks, the Feast of Booths, and the Feast of Unleavened Bread.

It was also the basis for the jubilee year, literally, "the year of the ram's horn" (Lev. 25:8–12). This was the last year in a cycle of fifty years. In this year, ushered in by the blast of the ram's horn from which it gets its name, prisoners were freed and all property returned to the original owner or to the owner's family as a reminder that no one really "owned" land except God. Although there is no evidence that the jubilee year and its rules were ever put into practice, it nevertheless remains a powerful statement of the belief that the land belongs to God and not to its human tenants.

THE LAND

Although the Israelites had been looking forward eagerly to settling down in "a land of milk and honey," in actuality it was not an easy process. Two major factors made gardening difficult: the limitations imposed by rainfall and the fact that the best farmland, along the coastal areas and river valleys, was already occupied by the Canaanites, who guarded these areas from their heavily fortified cities. The Israelites, forced to settle in the hill country, developed the ingenious method of terrace farming, which is still practiced today.

What was this "land of milk and honey" (an expression used eighteen times in the Old Testament) really like? It has not substantially changed during the last four thousand years, except for the spreading of the deserts because of deforestation and removal of plant cover. Its terrain is diverse. One writer suggests that one reason the Bible makes sense to people all over the earth is that it "so nearly runs the gamut of the world's climates, land forms, and living conditions."[2]

The land has four distinct geographical areas:

1. The coastal plain, where most of the grain is grown and where the Philistines lived, from whose name is derived the word *Palestine*. Through this area ran a trade route that was controlled by the Egyptians for many years. Solomon threatened Egypt's control of this route. The resulting conflict contributed to the split in the kingdom, when Egypt backed Jeroboam's revolt against Solomon in order to regain control of this important trade route.
2. The mountainous spine that runs between the coastal plains and rift valley. This was the center of Israelite territory. It includes the hill country in the north, which has the highest rainfall and is the most fertile, as well as the triangular desert in the south called the Negev, which figured in the wilderness wanderings of the Israelites.
3. The rift valley that splits Palestine in half by connecting the Sea of Galilee and the Dead Sea along the Jordan River. Biblical writers call it the Arabah.
4. The Transjordan plateau, which is mostly desert and rock and plays a relatively small part in biblical history. A part of it formed the land of Edom, the enemy of Israel.

The climate in Palestine is the same now as it was in ancient times. It varies from temperate with some rain in the north to subtropical and extremely dry in the south. There are two rains, autumn and spring. The first, the autumn rains, usually fall in October, followed by a mild, rainy winter and the spring rains in March. The heaviest rains are in December and January, which means that these winter months are the best months for crops; in the summer the intense heat dries up the vegetation. It is never extremely cold but rather is moderate enough for people to be comfortable out of doors most of the year.

In biblical times, the sowing of crops such as barley and wheat had to wait until after the autumn rains began because the ground was so hard from the summer heat and dryness. It was important that this rain came at the right time or the plants would not have enough time to mature before the summer heat set in. It was also a problem if the rains came too early, because the seeds planted would not receive another rain in time to encourage good growth. The promise of these rains was an important part of the covenant:

> If you will only heed his every commandment that I am commanding you today—loving the LORD your God, and serving him with all your heart and with all your soul—then he will give the rain for your land in its season, the early rain and the later rain, and you will gather in your grain, your wine, and your oil; and he will give grass in your fields for your livestock, and you will eat your fill.
>
> (Deut. 11:13–14)

The prophets also spoke of the coming of the rain as a sign of God's faithfulness. Joel cries out, "O children of Zion, be glad and rejoice in the LORD your God; for he has given the early rain for your vindication, he has poured down for you abundant rain, the early and the later rain, as before" (Joel 2:23).

To compensate for the unpredictability of rain, the Israelites developed runoff farming, that is, water-catching systems that directed runoff water by walls and channels into cisterns, from which it could be released into the terraced fields. This technique was used by King Uzziah in the eighth century B.C. to bring water even to the Negev desert.[3]

THE FIELDS

The most important crops grown in the mountain terraces and the coastal plains were grains. These staple crops included wheat in rainy areas and barley in semi-arid parts and the valleys of the desert. The domestication of grains dates back as far as 7000 B.C. in the Near East and was an important factor in the establishment of permanent villages. As wheat and barley became major nutritional sources, people were able to make the life change from hunting and gathering to farming.[4] Wheat and barley were among the "seven blessings," the crops promised to the Israelites by God (Deut. 8:8) when they entered the land where they would "eat bread without scarcity" (Deut. 8:9). Barley was considered much inferior to wheat but did not require as much water. It was probably the "standing grain" of the Philistines that Samson set on fire (Judg. 15:5). Other grains included millet, sorghum, *pannag,* spelt or rye, and hyssop, a tall plant with a seed head so large that one can feed an entire family. It was this hyssop stalk, not that of the smaller, medicinal herb with the same name, on which the sponge was raised to Jesus on the cross.

Planting was hard work. First the ground had to be cleared of rocks and stones, and then it was plowed by using a team of oxen and a plow with a conical blade. The early plows scratched the surface to a depth of only three to five inches, which explains why the farmer in the parable of the sower (Mark 4:3–8) did not realize he was sowing his seeds on rocky ground. Farmers plowed long, straight furrows to mark the place for sowing the seed. Sowing was done right away before these furrows disappeared. Often it was the women who sowed the seed, as planting was a family affair. Even the children helped in the fields.

Sowing was usually done by the broadcast method. Seeds were carried in a small bag from which the farmer would scoop handfuls to scatter in the furrows. After sowing the seeds, the farmer plowed again to turn the earth over the seeds.

Psalm 126:5–6 speaks of "sowing in tears." Perhaps this is a metaphor for the stress and strain of the planting season: the uncertainty of the rains, the hard labor of clearing land and plowing, the possibility of crop failure and of pests and disease, and the threat of weeds and of birds pilfering the seeds or the burgeoning grain. Gardening can be a matter of anxiety, particularly when one's life depends on its success.

The grains were planted during the early rains (mid-November to mid-January), and the summer crops—millet, sesame, lentils, cucumbers, and other vegetables—were planted from mid-January to mid-March. Harvesting took place in spring and summer. Barley was first, with wheat following a couple of weeks later, April at the earliest. Grain was harvested with a sickle, a curved iron blade with a wooden handle. The grain was then gathered into bundles called sheaves and taken to the threshing floor for winnowing and sieving, so that the chaff could be separated from the grain.[5] Grain was stored in large pottery jars or in stone-lined sunken granaries. Rows of these jars have been found in Jericho, with carbonized grain in them dating back to the time of the patriarchs.

THE ORCHARDS

Although grain was basic to daily needs, fruit trees were the most important element of the agricultural economy. They were usually grown in orchards, although grapes and figs were also grown close to homes. The sides of the house provided the extra warmth that enabled the grapes to ripen properly. Poetry and song celebrate fruit trees, which symbolized prosperity and peace. As the children of Israel entered the Promised Land, they were forbidden by law to cut down fruit trees (Deut. 20:19). A law also prohibited the picking of fruit from a tree for the first three years. In the fourth year, all the fruit was to be sold for the work of God, and only in the fifth year could the gardeners enjoy the fruit themselves (Lev. 19:23–25). A tenth of all fruit that was harvested was given to God (Lev. 27:30).

The three most important fruits for the Israelites were figs, grapes, and olives. All three are listed among the "seven blessings" (Deut. 8:8). The description of the peace and prosperity enjoyed under Solomon illustrates their importance in the lives of the people: "During Solomon's lifetime Judah and Israel lived in safety, . . . all of them under their vines and fig trees" (1 Kings 4:25). Micah also refers to the time of peace when "all [shall] sit under their own vines and under their own fig trees" (Micah 4:4).

The grapevine is referred to more than two hundred times in the Bible and was used as a symbol for the people of Israel by the prophets in the Old Testament (see Jer. 2:21), and in the New Testament by Christ as a symbol of himself (John 15:1). It was regarded as the national emblem of the Israelites and appeared on pottery, furniture, tombs, and coins. Planting a vineyard and enjoying its fruit were so important that a law stipulated one could not go to war before enjoying the fruit of one's vineyard (Deut. 20:6; 28:30). The grape harvest was a season of laughter and happiness. Judges 9:27 gives a description of how the people "went out into the field and gathered the grapes from their vineyards, trod them, and celebrated."

A vineyard demanded a lot of work. It needed constant weeding, pruning, spraying, watering, and fertilizing. In addition, walls and a watchtower had to be built for protection from thieves and wild animals, such as the "little foxes that ruin

the vineyards" mentioned in S. Sol. 2:15. And finally came the labor of picking. Because of this, it is easy to understand the bitter disappointment and frustration of the gardener who asks in Isaiah 5:

> What more was there to do for my vineyard
>   that I have not done in it?
> When I expected it to yield grapes,
>   why did it yield wild grapes?
>
> (Isa. 5:4)

Pruning was done in spring after the plant blossomed and again after the harvest. The pruning ensured that the plant's energy would produce rich fruit instead of prolific vines and leaves and thick stems. Jesus drew on this image when he referred to God's pruning those who bear fruit so they will be even more productive (John 15:2). Grapes were harvested in August and September. Although most farmers harvested their own grapes, the wealthy sublet their vineyards for a share in the harvest. Grapes were eaten fresh, dried into raisins, and made into wine.

The fig tree was also significant in the life of the Israelites, as testified to by the more than forty references to figs in the Bible. The fig tree provided two ample harvests a year, and it offered welcome shade because of its thick foliage and great height; some grow as tall as thirty feet. Figs were especially important because they could be dried and stored to be eaten out of season. Dried figs dating from 5000 B.C. have been discovered in Judea.

The most important tree cultivated in Palestine in biblical times, however, was the olive. One tree could supply a family with all the fats necessary for cooking, lighting, and making soap. Olives, along with a crust of bread, formed the daily food for laborers and travelers. So respected was the olive tree that its oil was also used for anointing kings and priests, for treating the sick, for temple lamps, and as a solvent for spices, incense, and aromatics. Its wood was also prized for wooden ornaments and household utensils.[6] The olive leaf has symbolized peace, new life, and hope since Noah's time. It was used as a metaphor for righteous people and for the children of Israel. Olive trees have been known to bear fruit for a thousand years, so when Hosea likens the beauty of Israel to that of the olive tree, it is likely that he has in mind its fruitfulness, not its physical splendor (Hos. 14:6). It is difficult to eradicate an old olive, as shoots will continue to spring up from its roots (see Job 14:7–9). In fact, the psalmist compares children to "olive shoots" springing up around one's table (Ps. 128:3).

Most of the olive crop was used to make olive oil. This was done by first crushing the olives in a shallow basin cut in rock. Then the crushed olives were pressed to extract the oil. Gethsemane (which means "the place of the oil presses") was not a garden in the modern sense but a walled olive orchard, whose thick shade provided a welcome respite from the heat of the noonday sun. It is very likely that it derived its name from the press or presses that stood within its walls. Such gardens are still common in the Near East.

Other fruits grown in biblical times include the pomegranate (also mentioned in the "seven blessings" in Deuteronomy); the sycamine, or black mulberry; the date palm; the "apple" (which most botanists identify with the apricot); and the sycamore fig. The sycamore fig has been an important food among the poor of the Near East since prehistoric times, although it is much inferior to the common fig. No one ate it who could afford anything better. When Amos said he was a gatherer of sycamore figs ("a dresser of sycamore trees," Amos 7:14), he was describing himself as being among the poorest of the poor.

Orchards also included nut trees: pistachio, almond, and walnut, and possibly hazelnuts and chestnuts (see S. Sol. 6:11). Josephus, a Jewish historian who lived in and wrote about the first century A.D., describes the widespread cultivation of walnut trees in Palestine at that time.

THE HOUSEHOLD GARDEN

Most of the "gardens" mentioned in scripture are associated with the wealthy. However, it was not uncommon for households to have vegetable garden plots, although they were woefully lacking in the variety possible to us today. Of the 110 plants named in the Bible, very few were grown for food. Plants grown in these gardens usually fell into four groups: (1) vegetables—leeks, onions, and garlic; (2) pulses—red lentils, broad beans, chickpeas, and garden peas; (3) gourds—watermelon, muskmelon, cucumber, and bottle gourds; and (4) spices—coriander, cumin, black cumin or fitches, black mustard, dill, hyssop, mint, rue, saffron, caper bush, wormwood, fenugreek, and mustard.

People apparently depended on wild vegetation for variety in their diet. The term *grass of the field* may refer to edible herbs, pot herbs, and other plants that people picked along the streams and in the fields. These probably included mallow, dwarf chicory, garden rocket, and the "bitter herbs" that formed a part of the Passover meal: lettuce, parsley, horseradish, endive, watercress, sorrel, and dandelions. These were also eaten as salad. Some of these may have been grown in household gardens as well.

Household gardens may have been laid out in chessboard patterns, with each plot separated by shallow furrows, copying a system learned in Egypt. They were watered "by foot," meaning that water was diverted from a central channel into the furrows by removing dirt with the foot. Deuteronomy 11:10 describes this system but reminds the Israelites they will not have to depend on it in they same way they did in Egypt, because they will be entering a land "watered by rain from the sky, a land that the LORD your God looks after."

ROYAL GARDENS

It is in the books of Esther and Song of Solomon that we find descriptions of the luxurious royal gardens. In Esther (1:6) there is a description of a garden surrounded with white and blue hangings, fastened with purple linen cords to silver rings around marble pillars. The pavements were of marble, and there were couches of gold and silver. It may have been that these courtyard gardens led to the hunting park of the king.

The garden described in the Song of Solomon (4:12–16; 5:1; 6:11) gives us our clearest picture of the lavish beauty of the royal gardens associated with Solomon.

The exact location of this famous garden is not known, but it is believed to have been near the palace. It is mentioned in 2 Kings 25:4. The garden described in the Song of Solomon apparently was enclosed, grew lilies and other flowers, and included a garden of nut trees and a garden of spices. Among these spices were not only local ones but also others that may have come from Arabia and India. Josephus says that Solomon "was not unacquainted with any of the natures of his plants, nor did he omit to make inquiries about them, but described them all like a philosopher, and demonstrated his excellent knowledge of their several properties."[7] This is confirmed in 1 Kings 4:33: "He would speak of trees, from the cedar that is in the Lebanon to the hyssop that grows in the wall; he would speak of animals, and birds, and reptiles, and fish."

Other plants that may have grown in the royal garden were camphire and saffron, aloes, spikenard, ginger grass, balm, oleander, Phoenician roses, and water lilies. Solomon seems to have made collections of plants from all parts of the world, especially of the scented plants that played such an important part in Oriental gardens. Biblical scholar A. W. Anderson comments, "The gardens of many eastern lands have not changed very much since the days of King Solomon. Then as now the provision of shade and water, luscious fruits and aromatic herbs were matters of prime importance and little attention was paid to flowers."[8]

A FINAL WORD

Except for the very wealthy, biblical people did gardening not so much for pleasure as for sustenance. And yet as people planted, watered, weeded, and harvested, they did not forget who the real Gardener was, and they sang songs of thanksgiving and praise to God with words like those in Psalm 104:

> You cause the grass to grow for the cattle,
>   and plants for people to use,
> to bring forth food from the earth
>   and wine to gladden the human heart,
> oil to make the face shine,
>   and bread to strengthen the human heart.
> . . . .
> These all look to you
>   to give them their food in due season;
> when you give to them, they gather it up;
>   when you open your hand, they are filled with good things.
>   (Ps. 104:14–15, 27–28)

FOR SPIRITUAL GROWTH

1. If we truly believed "the land belongs to God," how would it affect our attitudes toward ownership of property? Toward ecology? Toward gardening?

2. The Israelites gave a tenth of all their harvest to God. List some ways in which we could practice tithing the harvest of our gardens.

3. God promised the people of Israel "seven blessings" when they entered the Promised Land. Make a list of seven blessings God has given you, and write a prayer of thanksgiving for these.

2 THE GARDEN OF THE LORD

Nourishment for Body and Soul

And the LORD God planted a garden in Eden.
—Genesis 2:8

The earth is the LORD's and all that is in it,
    the world, and those who live in it.
—Psalm 24:1

All through the long winter I dream of my garden. On the first warm day of Spring
I dig my fingers deep into the soft earth. I can feel its energy and my spirits soar.
—Helen Hayes

Be it ours to meditate
In these calm shades Thy milder majesty,
And to the beautiful order of Thy works
Learn to conform the order of our lives.
        —William Cullen Bryant

O Thou, who kindly dost provide
For every creature's want!
We bless Thee, God of nature wide,
For all Thy goodness lent;
And, if it please Thee, heavenly guide,
May never worse be sent;

> But whether granted or denied,
> Lord, bless us with content!
> —Robert Burns

It all began in Eden. In the four words "God planted a garden" (Gen. 2:8) is a foundational biblical truth: it is God who is the master gardener. It is God who plants, whose initiating power brings into being the world that is our home, our garden. The real gardener is neither the farmer who grows acres and acres of wheat nor the garden club president noted for her roses but the Creator of the universe, the one who "laid the foundation of the earth" (Job. 38:4). The people of God in the Old Testament understood this clearly. In the Old Testament, God is always depicted as the one who plans and plants a garden for human beings, by means of which God "satisfies the thirsty, and the hungry he fills with good things" (Ps. 107:9). As Walter Brueggemann has recognized, "The destiny of the human creature is to live in God's world, not a world of his/her own making. The human creation is to live with God's other creatures, some of which are dangerous, but all of which are to be ruled and cared for. The destiny of the human creature is to live in God's world, with God's other creatures, on God's terms."[1]

Not only is this Garden carefully planned and planted but it is also sustained by the constant care of the faithful Gardener, who waters it, nourishes it, prunes and weeds it, and finally brings it to joyful harvest.

The metaphor of God as gardener is a rich one, with many levels of meaning. In scripture it is used not only to picture God's creative activity in the world of nature but also to describe God's sovereignty over history, found in God's planting and "plucking up" whole nations. In addition, it pictures the covenant love God has for human beings, a love that sustains and nourishes them. It is a metaphor that reveals to us much about God's nature: about God as creator, as sustainer, as life-giver, as lover. It illumines and informs the doctrines of creation, providence, and the sovereignty of God. As we begin to reflect on the image of the Gracious Gardener, these doctrines become more than just empty words. They find concretization in ways that capture our imaginations and hearts. The doctrine of creation reminds us that "the earth is the Lord's," a garden that belongs to God. When we abuse and misuse this Garden, we are "trespassing," committing an offense against the garden's Owner. The doctrine of providence is clarified when we remember that it describes a Gardener who does not neglect but protects, defends, and preserves the Garden and its inhabitants. The sovereignty of God is best understood by looking at God's acts of love and justice in the world: planning, planting, watering, pruning, harvesting. Scripture tells us again and again how God the Gardener goes about these tasks. These passages instruct us not only about God's activities but about what the Gardener expects from us.

GOD PLANS

Before I planted my herb garden a few years ago, I drew up a plan of the vision that was in my head. I designed its shape; I consulted herb books for lists of herbs that do well in the South. I dreamed ambitious dreams of the herbs I'd never even seen and penciled their wonderful names in on my plan: elecampane, pennyroyal, costmary, and dittany of Crete. And slowly, year by year, my garden came into being. It was not quite the same as my dreams (I never did locate any elecampane or dittany of Crete), but it came into being because of a plan, an intention.

God also works according to plan. In John Calvin's words, "All events are governed by God's secret plan."[2] Seeds are being planted all the time, according to a great and wonderful design of which we catch only fleeting glimpses. We are all part of an enormous, complex, formal garden, whose pattern, as with most gardens, we see more clearly at completion than while it is still in the process of unfolding. As C. S. Lewis wrote in a letter to Sheldon Vanauken:

> And indeed, we can't suppose God saying (as a human artist might) "That effect, though it has turned out rather well, was, I must admit, no part of my original design." Then the total act of creation, including *our own* creation (which is going on all the time) meets us, doesn't it? in every event at every moment: the act of a Person dealing with persons and knowing what He does.[3]

It is planning that distinguishes a well-ordered garden from a field of wild-flowers. The shape of its rows or beds, the careful decisions about "companion crops" or color contrasts, the attention to the size of full-grown plants and the space they will need—all of these are the marks of a garden and reveal a plan in the mind of the gardener. By looking at a garden and the way it is planned and planted, we learn something about the one who designed it. Was a utilitarian mind at work, so that more attention was given to production of edible crops than to landscaping? Or is there an aesthetic sensibility at work in the lavish display of brilliant annuals against the muted gray-greens of the herbs? Calvin expressed much the same idea when he wrote that the "skillful ordering of the universe is for us a sort of mirror in which we can contemplate God, who is otherwise invisible."[4] In other words, the garden plan of creation teaches us about the Gardener.

What do we learn about the Gardener by looking at the Garden? We learn that God delights in the intricacies of interconnectedness, those mysterious links between soil, plants, animals, light, and water about which we are constantly learning more and more. We learn that "our ways are not God's ways": there are mysteries in the Garden we cannot fathom. We learn that there are Garden rules and that breaking those rules results in calamity. We learn that God has not abandoned the Garden but keeps and sustains it.

This is brought home to us in the delightful parable of the farmers in Isa. 28:23–29, where God is the master gardener who teaches farmers how to farm according to a well thought-out plan. They know when to plow and when to plant. They understand that dill is to be broadcast and wheat planted in orderly rows. Barley is planted "in its proper place," and spelt is used in borders. Threshing also is done according to a careful plan, with one method for dill and cumin and another for the bread grains. The parable makes it clear that the farmer's success comes from listening to the advice of God the Master Gardener, who is "wonderful in counsel, and excellent in wisdom" (Isa. 28:29) and who teaches farmers what they need to know. Isaiah paints a sharp contrast between this careful farmer, who learns how to plan by listening to God, and the priests and prophets who "err in vision" and "stumble in giving judgment" (28:7) because they are no longer listening to and learning from God.

The Master Gardener is not only a master planner but a master teacher. To know the Gardener's plan for our lives, to develop gardening skills ourselves, we have only to listen to that Teacher. "Morning by morning he wakens—wakens my ear to listen as those who are taught" (Isa. 50:4).

GOD PLANTS

But planning is not enough to bring a garden into being. There is also the hard work of preparation: tilling the soil, adding nutrients, removing weeds and rubble, and, finally, planting. Throughout the Bible, the planting metaphor is used in a variety of ways to describe the mystery of how God acts in the world. By examining this variety of meanings, we gain a deeper understanding of how the people of God responded to "God's wonderful works."

God Plants in the Events of History

Biblical references to God as an intentional, orderly planter extend beyond God's planning for the created world around us. In fact, in most cases the metaphor is used for God's sovereignty over history: planting, transplanting, and uprooting entire nations. It is used particularly to express God's purposeful dealings with Israel. In 2 Sam. 7:10 (repeated in 1 Chron. 17:9) there is a marvelous description of what Walter Brueggemann describes as the "powerful, relentless graciousness"[5] of God toward Israel: "And I will appoint a place for my people Israel and will plant them, so that they may live in their own place, and be disturbed no more; and evildoers shall afflict them no more, as formerly."

These words are a part of God's promise to establish the house of David as a dynasty through which the "throne of his kingdom" will be established forever. God is offering a permanency, a plantedness far greater than that symbolized by the temple David planned to build. David's response is one of sheer exultation, rejoicing in that graciousness: "For you, O Lord GOD, have spoken, and with your blessing shall the house of your servant be blessed forever" (2 Sam. 7:29b).

Psalms and Isaiah provide even more explicit descriptions of God as a gardener whose work has been richly successful, producing "vines" (the symbol of fecundity and growth) by bringing a shoot from Egypt, planting it, and clearing the ground for it, where "it took deep root and filled the land," as the psalmist says (Ps. 80:9). This image of Israel as a vine was much loved by the prophets and poets.

Isaiah has two very different "songs of the vineyard." In the first, Isa. 5:1–7, there is a graphic picture of a vineyard that disappointed its Gardener: it yielded wild grapes, in spite of all the Gardener had done for it, tilling the soil, clearing away stones, planting the best vines, even providing a watchtower and a wine vat. The poem ends on a note of judgment:

> For the vineyard of the LORD of hosts
>   is the house of Israel,
> and the people of Judah
>   are his pleasant planting;
> he expected justice,
>   but saw bloodshed;
> righteousness,
>   but heard a cry!
>
> (Isa. 5:7)

The second Song of the Vineyard (Isa. 27:2–6), however, is quite different. Here, God is a protective gardener, who cares fiercely about the vineyard that grew from the "shoot from Egypt" and who has a plan for the vineyard:

> On that day:
> A pleasant vineyard, sing about it!
>   I, the LORD, am its keeper;
>   every moment I water it.
> I guard it night and day
>   so that no one can harm it;
>   I have no wrath.
> . . . .
> In days to come Jacob shall take root,
>   Israel shall blossom and put forth shoots,
>   and fill the whole world with fruit.
>
> (Isa. 27:2–3, 6)

In the first song, Israel became a field of thorns and briers because it did not listen to the Gardener. In the second, the Gardener is willing to defend the vineyard against "thorns and briers," which are its enemies, and will make it a blessing to the whole earth.

It was the prophet Jeremiah, though, who was particularly fond of the "planting" image. For him, the garden was an expression of the covenant relationship between God and Israel: "I will make an everlasting covenant with them, never to draw back from doing good to them; and I will put the fear of me in their hearts, so that they may not turn from me. I will rejoice in doing good to them, and I will plant them in this land in faithfulness, with all my heart and all my soul" (Jer. 32:40–41).

This beautiful picture can be understood by every faithful gardener who yearns over the tender green seedlings and the tiny grains of wheat with "heart and soul," who protects them from harsh sun and drought, who hoes and weeds and "rejoices in doing good to them." In my own desire to be a heart-and-soul gardener, I read gardening books about companion planting and when to set out broccoli and peppers. When one herb bed proved too rich for my sage plants, I moved them to sandier soil. When the thyme was overshadowed by the six-foot-tall pineapple sage bushes, I revised my beds. All summer I water, root out the weeds, and remove tomato worms and slugs. In the winter I mulch beds with newspaper and grass clippings and build up my compost heap with household garbage, manure, and leaves. If I want to be faithful to my garden, I can never stop giving care to the soil and the plants. In the same way, God never draws back from doing good to the people of the covenant. God plants with faithfulness, enthusiasm, and devotion and cares with heart and soul for the Garden and those who people it.

In Jeremiah 31, the prophet uses the "gardener" image to remind those in exile that God is indeed the overseer of their destiny, who will restore them to their homeland:

> They shall come and sing aloud on the height of Zion,
>   and they shall be radiant over the goodness of the LORD,
> over the grain, the wine, and the oil,
>   and over the young of the flock and the herd;

> their life shall become like a watered garden,
>   and they shall never languish again.
>   (Jer. 31:12)

But as in the first Song of the Vineyard in Isaiah, there is a stern warning in the planting metaphor. When my brussels sprouts refused to produce an edible crop, I pulled them up and threw them on the compost heap. In the same way, if the Garden planted by God is not productive, then it will be "plucked up, broken down, and destroyed" (see Jer. 31:28). This idea is vividly expressed in the famous "potter and clay" passage of Jeremiah 18. The prophet shifts from the metaphor of the potter to that of the gardener: "And at another moment I may declare concerning a nation or a kingdom that I will build and plant it, but if it does evil in my sight, not listening to my voice, then I will change my mind about the good that I had intended to do to it" (18:9).

Although God has a plan and an intention, like every gardener, God is constantly, as Calvin said, "making new beginnings, opening up new possibilities, initiating new events."[6] The same idea is reflected in God's stern warning to the remnant in Judah not to flee to Egypt: "If you will only remain in this land, then I will build you up and not pull you down, I will plant you, and not pluck you up; for I am sorry for the disaster that I have brought upon you" (Jer. 42:10).

This passage bears a strong resemblance to John 15:1–6, in which Jesus describes the fruitless branches that will be burned by the "vinegrower," or in another translation, "the gardener." In the covenant context, it means that passionately dedicated gardeners have expectations of response and fruitfulness from their gardens. The covenant promise "I will be your God" is connected to a commitment: "You will be my people." Our Gardener expects good fruit from our vines, not sour, wild grapes.

Jesus also used the vineyard image to make it clear that some plantings are not God's. In Matt. 15:13, when told by the disciples that the Pharisees have taken offense at his words, Jesus replies, "Every plant that my heavenly Father has not planted will be uprooted." In contrast to God's carefully planned and planted vineyard, Israel (represented here by its ruling class, the Pharisees) has become "thorns and briers." It has failed to bear good fruit and will be uprooted.

Jesus' parable in Luke 13:6–9 employs another Old Testament image for Israel: the fig tree. "Like the first fruit on the fig tree, in its first season, I saw your ancestors" (Hos 9:10). The parable of the barren fig tree in Luke reminds us that God is a gardener who offers grace. The gardener in the parable begs the owner of the barren fig tree to give a "stay of execution" until the tree has been fertilized for a year. It's the only place in scripture where manure is a symbol of grace, but every good gardener knows what a blessing manure can be. What began as an announcement of judgment has become a call to repentance. If the fig tree of Israel responds to the manure of grace, then all will be "well and good."

All these references remind us of God's sovereign role in history. The world is indeed in God's hands. We cannot understand all that is happening. Like ants in a cornfield, we can see only our tiny bit of crumbling soil and the base of the cornstalk before us. We have little idea of the ears of corn coming to fruition around us, to say nothing of the size and extent of the whole cornfield. But faith does not mean having access to the whole garden design; it means being faithful farmers who garden according to the wisdom and insight provided us from the one who made the design.

God Plants the Word

One of the most vivid pictures of God the Gardener in the New Testament is in the parable of the sower (Mark 4:3–8). The parable is best understood when we remember how planting was done in Jesus' day. The soil was plowed shallowly, then the farmer walked across the fields, broadcasting the seeds by hand. Often underneath a thin layer of soil lay a broad sheet of shale. There were hardened paths made by small animals or by people crisscrossing the fields. Birds swooped down and ate the seeds before they could be turned under the soil. The ubiquitous thorns and obnoxious darnel (see chapter 5) sprang up thickly around the struggling plants.

Jesus had undoubtedly watched this process many times before he used it in a parable, and so he was able to paint a vivid picture of the sower generously scattering the seed across the waiting soil. The parable is about God the Gardener sowing the seed of the word, of the good news of the kingdom. What grows from that seed has a lot to do with the kind of soil onto which it falls. Is it rich and loamy, or dry and hard? Is it choked by weeds and briers, or cluttered with rocks and stones?

Good gardeners know the qualities of good soil: there must be a proper pH balance (not too much acidity or alkalinity), it must be adequately mulched, and it must be friable. "Friable" means loose and crumbly, not hard-packed like my South Carolina red clay. It means soil that is receptive, that allows room for the roots of the seed to grow and develop. It is this kind of receptivity that James was thinking of when he too spoke of the word being planted: "Welcome with meekness the implanted word that has the power to save your souls. But be doers of the word, and not merely hearers who deceive themselves" (James 1:21b–22).

The word *meekness* means the opposite of pride. It describes an attitude of complete dependence on God. It can be translated as "humility" or "gentleness" or "perfect courtesy," but perhaps the best interpretation is biblical scholar William Barclay's phrase "a teachable spirit." James is speaking not of soil that is passive but rather of that which is filled with the energy of expectancy. He gives us a picture of a garden that is ready for seed, confident in its complete dependence on the Gardener, in its belief that the seed will be good and that it has a role to play in the growth of that seed.

The soil does not generate the seed; the seed is the gift of grace. The soil receives the seed with hope and eager expectation and perfect courtesy and gratitude. God is the giver. We are thanks-givers.

The seed that God "implants" and that we are to nourish and bring to life is the word itself. This seed, when planted in receptive, "teachable" soil, will blossom and flower and bear fruit. What kind of fruit? The New Testament has a funny idea about productivity. It never uses the world's standards of fruitfulness: salaries, degrees, honors, material possessions. Instead, it speaks of good works and increasing in the knowledge of God (Col. 1:10); of love, joy, and peace (Gal. 5:22); of righteousness (Phil. 1:11); and of lips that acknowledge God's name (Heb. 13:15).

A garden motto reads:

Kind hearts are the garden;
Kind thoughts are the roots,

> Kind words are the blossoms,
> Kind deeds are the fruits.

This is an appropriate statement of the fruits that will grow in our gardens when we receive the word implanted by God. And the seeds from those fruits are gathered by God to be planted in other lives, for other harvests.

GOD SUSTAINS AND NOURISHES

Nourishment for the Body

In the very first chapter of the Bible, God's loving care is shown by the provision of food: "God said, 'See, I have given you every plant yielding seed that is upon the face of all the earth. . . . everything that has the breath of life, I have given every green plant for food' "(Gen. 1:29, 30b). It was this thoughtful recognition of human physical needs to which Jesus referred in the Sermon on the Mount when he reminded his listeners, "Your heavenly Father knows that you need all these things" (Matt. 6:32b).

Food was an integral part of the covenant God made with the Israelites. To a nomadic people, the following promise would have sounded like a return to the garden in Eden:

> If you follow my statutes and keep my commandments and observe them faithfully, I will give you your rains in their season, and the land shall yield its produce, and the trees of the field shall yield their fruit. Your threshing shall overtake the vintage, and the vintage shall overtake the sowing; you shall eat your bread to the full, and live securely in the land. And I will grant peace in the land, and you shall lie down, and no one shall make you afraid.
>
> (Lev. 26:3–6)

This assurance that God would provide a garden for them was the message of hope that kept the Israelites going. It was the promise of shalom, which meant not only peace but joy, well-being, contentment, a full belly, all needs satisfied—ice cream on top of chocolate-amaretto brownies. The garden represented a promise of God's continuing love and care.

Nowhere is this promise of well-being more clearly related to the satisfaction of physical needs than in the description of the "good land" that God promised Israel in Deuteronomy 8. Here, God's providential care is spelled out in terms of "flowing streams" and the seven blessings: wheat, barley, vines, fig trees, pomegranates, olive trees, and honey. The Gardener's promise to these hungry wanderers is one of sustenance and fullness: "You shall eat your fill and bless the LORD your God for the good land that he has given you" (Deut. 8:10).

The Psalms are rich with references to God's gardening activity. There are prayers to God for "abundance of grain in the land" (Ps. 72:16) and that "barns be filled, with produce of every kind" (144:13). There are words of praise: "The eyes of all look to you, and you give them their food in due season" (145:15) and "Happy are those whose help is the God of Jacob, . . . who gives food to the hungry" (146:5, 7). In Psalm 147, God provides not only for human beings but for all creatures:

> Sing to the LORD with thanksgiving;
>   make melody to our God on the lyre.
> He covers the heavens with clouds,
>   prepares rain for the earth,
>   makes grass grow on the hills.
> He gives to the animals their food,
>   and to the young ravens when they cry.
>   (Ps. 147:7–9)

This psalm begins with words of praise for the God who is sovereign not only over the lives of the Israelites but over all of the created world. In verses 7 through 9, the psalmist reminds us that the sovereign God who created the whole world is the same saving, caring God who has always provided for it.

In the New Testament also, God is pictured as the provider of nourishment. In the Lord's Prayer there is the petition "Give us this day our daily bread" (Matt. 6:11), and in the Sermon on the Mount, Jesus reminds his followers not to worry about food or drink or clothing, because the heavenly Father who feeds the birds will feed them too (Matt. 6:26). In 2 Cor. 9:10, Paul refers to God as "he who supplies seed to the sower and bread for food." In each case, God is the one who not only knows our physical needs but shows loving care and concern in meeting those needs.

This steadfast love and care is described in the Old Testament with the Hebrew word *hesed*. The word can be translated as "loving-kindness," "mercy," "goodness," or even "grace." More than anything else, however, it means "covenant love." It is a combination of steadfast love and loyalty, and it describes God's persistent love for the covenant people. We do not deserve it, but it will not let us go.

The Old Testament response to this *hesed* is always praise and thanksgiving. This praise for *hesed* is a recurrent theme in the Psalms. "The LORD is good to all, and his compassion is over all that he has made. . . . My mouth will speak the praise of the LORD, and all flesh will bless his holy name forever and ever" (Ps. 145:9, 21). In other passages thanksgiving is the dominant note, as in Ps. 136:1: "O give thanks to the LORD, for he is good, for his steadfast love endures forever."

In these lines from "Prayer for a Vegetable Garden," a contemporary expression of thanksgiving, poet Robert Jones praises God's goodness:

> But then I taste a tomato that tastes tomato.
> I pick the ripened corn
> and plop it into a pot of boiling water.
> I slice the fresh zucchinis, snap the beans,
> and sit down to a feast of flavors
> that must be like the feasts in Eden
> before the serpent said a word.
> So I thank you for this garden, God,
> and for the strength to tend it in my way,
> and for my tiny harvest,
> and for the tang and savor of each bite.[7]

God Nourishes the Soul

Genesis 2 adds another dimension of the garden to that of sustenance: pleasure. The garden in Eden contained "every tree that is pleasant to the sight and good for food" (Gen. 2:9). The name Eden itself means "delight," and the term *Eden* became a symbol for the prophets of all that is both sustaining and pleasurable:

> For the LORD will comfort Zion;
>   he will comfort all her waste places,
> and will make her wilderness like Eden,
>   her desert like the garden of the LORD;
> joy and gladness will be found in her,
>   thanksgiving and the voice of song.
>   (Isa. 51:3)

> Before them the land is like the garden of Eden,
>   but after them a desolate wilderness.
>   (Joel 2:3b)

In later, rabbinic thought, the garden of Eden formed the basis for descriptions of paradise, the part of Sheol where the righteous went after death. The term *paradise* comes from the Persian word *pardes*, referring to a nobleman's walled garden or park. The vision of paradise as a garden is a very old concept in the Middle East. It is mentioned not only in the Bible but in the Koran as well. Paradise was always thought of as a place of shade and plenty, well watered and abundant, where all needs would be met, and eventually, it became synonymous with heaven.

Other scriptures, too, mention the pleasurable side of the garden. Psalm 104 celebrates God's creation of the world and the provision God has made for the needs of the creatures that live in it. But tucked away in verse 15 is a recognition that God also provides for human pleasure: for "wine to gladden the human heart, oil to make the face shine." Undoubtedly, though, the book of the Bible that best describes the pleasure gardens can give is the Song of Solomon. Not only does it use agricultural metaphors for the language of love—"His cheeks are like beds of spices, yielding fragrance" (S. Sol. 5:13)—but it has passages that celebrate pleasure in the beauty of the garden itself:

> My beloved has gone down to his garden,
>   to the beds of spices,

to pasture his flock in the gardens,
    and to gather lilies.
. . . .
I went down to the nut orchard,
    to look at the blossoms of the valley,
to see whether the vines had budded,
    whether the pomegranates were in bloom.
                                       (S. Sol. 6:2, 11)

Gardens like these provide nourishment for the soul, consolation for the heart, and inspiration for the mind. A wealthy southerner named Cason Callaway and his wife, Virginia, understood that such gardens are important. In the late 1940s, they decided to use their wealth to create a magnificent garden that would be open to everyone, instead of a private retreat for the Callaway family and their friends. Callaway chose a site in southern Georgia, land that had been abused by years of cotton farming. Today, thousands of people flock to beautiful Callaway Gardens, which has become a sanctuary not only for native plants and wildlife but for people as well.

There is sheer pleasure in simply walking through such beautiful gardens, enjoying the magnificence of trees, shrubs, splendid flowers, and herbs. Gardens like these bring delight to the senses with color, fragrances, textures, sounds. Edwina Gateley has beautifully expressed that delight:

> I feel like an integral part of the whole of creation. . . . I want to love and care for it because everything created is for my good and my joy. I stop to talk to the birds and the flowers. I fly with the butterflies, awed by the night, refreshed by the morning. I delight in the garden God has put before me. . . . Everything I see praises God just where it is, and I walk and run by it all—enjoying it all. This is my prayer, my hymn to God. This is my participation in creation—loving it, calling it to fulfillment, to be the delight of humanity.[8]

The mysterious restorative power of gardens is hard to explain, but many people have experienced their healing and solace. In her poignant diary, Anne Frank, hiding from the Germans during World War II in the "Secret Annex," wrote these words of longing:

The best remedy for those who are frightened, lonely or unhappy is to go outside, somewhere they can be alone, alone with the sky, nature and God. For then and only then can you feel that everything is as it should be and that God wants people to be happy amid nature's beauty and simplicity. As long as this exists, and that should be forever, I know that there will be solace for every sorrow, whatever the circumstances. I firmly believe that nature can bring comfort to all who suffer.[9]

I entered seminary as a "late bloomer," and during the long, hot summer of Greek school, after wrestling with torturous Greek verbs all day, I'd go to my garden for refreshment and renewal. Like Helen Hayes, I found that there was something about getting my hands in good, black earth, about clearing away weeds from my Swiss chard and tomatoes, that did my soul good. I felt connected to the real world again. I found a new sense of hope and energy in watching the progress of small, growing plants, and I delighted in my "participation in creation," to use Edwina Gateley's expression.

The healing power of the world around us has been documented in many ways. Doctors have discovered that patients recover more quickly from surgery when they can view trees, instead of walls and other people, through their hospital windows. Very ill people and the aged derive great psychological benefits from having a pet. Ralph Waldo Emerson wrote, "All my hurts my garden spade can heal. A woodland walk, a quest of river-grapes, a mocking thrush, a wild rose or rock-loving columbine, salve my worst wounds."[10]

In 1983, I was a staff associate for the General Assembly of the Presbyterian Church (U.S.A.). On my hour-long drive to the office in Atlanta, I had noticed many times a high knoll where a home had burned. Isolated on a country road, the knoll was deserted and still. Early one morning, on impulse, I turned into the drive leading to the top of the hill. Below me lay a vista of serene pastoral beauty: rolling fields, wooded groves, a small lake. A tiny tractor hummed in the distance, and bird calls filled the air. As I paused in the freshness, a sense of the presence of God filled me with wholeness, peace, shalom. It was a renewing time, a moment of reflection on the constant, guiding care of God's love.

Jesus knew the importance of times apart in the natural world for healing and renewal. He urged his disciples to "come away to a deserted place all by yourselves and rest a while" (Mark 6:30). He knew how worn out they were. Their lives were so caught up in the demands others made on their time and energy that they did not even have time to eat. "Come away," he said, "come away into the quiet healing of God's creation."

In the busy agendas of our contemporary life, "deserted places" seem hard to come by. Tight schedules, the demands of work and family life, the tensions and frustrations under which we live—all squeeze out times for just being quiet. The result is that tension breeds tension and pressure increases pressure until physical or mental breakdown and exhaustion occur. Times apart are not luxuries; they are essential. Vacations, weekends, holidays, and retreats are important, but we also need to find time in *each day's* schedule for reflection on God's wonderful works and recognition of God's presence in our lives. A park bench, a quiet room, or a serene spot on the side of the road can be our deserted place.

After the Last Supper, Jesus went, "as was his custom" (Luke 22:39), to a place John calls "a garden" and Matthew names "Gethsemane." Since its name means "oil press," it may have been a privately owned orchard with a press for squeezing oil from the olives. The exact location of Gethsemane is unknown, but it was apparently east of Jerusalem, beyond the brook Kidron near the Mount of Olives. John tells us Jesus went there frequently with his disciples (18:2). Perhaps it is not too much to suppose that they went there just as they went to the "deserted places": for peace and quiet, for prayer, and for the restoration of the soul.

Jesus needed strength and solace for what lay ahead, so he went to a garden. The poet Sidney Lanier describes him as "forspent with love and shame." It was not an easy time; his sweat was like drops of blood. But he was able to pray a healing prayer: "Not my will but thine be done." Lanier attributes this healing to the olives who "were not blind to him"; to the little gray leaves that "were kind to him"; to even the thorn-tree that "had a mind to him," so that he came out of the garden "content with death and shame."[11] Poetic license? Or a deep and true insight into the balm and healing we receive in the gardens of God?

In my basil bed there is a garden plaque that declares:

> The kiss of the sun for pardon,
> The song of the birds for mirth:
> One is nearer God's heart in a garden
> Than any place else on earth.

Now we in the Reformed tradition know the biblical evidence is that one comes a lot nearer to God's heart through obedience and love than by walking through basil beds. Nevertheless, these words have an element of truth. I suspect William Cullen Bryant was on the right track in the words quoted at the beginning of this chapter. The Garden around us teaches us about God's order and the need for that order in our lives. Perhaps both the pleasure and the restoration we experience come from an innate sense of God's *hesed*, God's covenant love, of which creation itself is a visible reminder.

The Eco-Justice Task Force of the Presbyterian Church (U.S.A.) published in 1989 an excellent and thoughtful study document, *Keeping and Healing the Creation*. In it are these words: "Creation is the theater of God's grace—receiving the loving kindness of God, given not just to people, but to all creatures. 'Nature', so integral and indispensable to human life, is both a recipient and a means of grace—the same grace we see most fully in Jesus Christ."[12]

I have experienced grace in my garden. It teaches me humility as I recognize the truth of Paul's phrase "Only God . . . gives the growth" (1 Cor. 3:7), no matter how faithful my planting and weeding and watering. It teaches me patience as I watch for the first tiny green shoots springing from almost invisible seed. It teaches me hope as I experience the cycle of the seasons and the loving care of the one who provides seedtime and harvest and gives us our daily bread.

A FINAL WORD

Genesis tells us that human life began in a garden. The Gospels tell us that Christ's resurrected life began in a garden. The garden is a beautiful symbol of the grace of beginnings and of new life. It is a symbol of the careful planning and planting of the Good Gardener, who deeply understands our need for healing and mysteriously restores both body and soul through the greening and flowering of the Garden in which we live.

FOR SPIRITUAL GROWTH

1. What does the image of God as gardener say to you about the character of God? What does the Gardener expect of you?

2. Think of yourself as a garden. What kind of soil are you? Are you hardened over with cynicism, inertia, anger, fear, or discouragement? Or do you have the "energy of expectancy" in your life and work? What are the "fruits of the spirit" your garden produces best? (See Gal. 5:22–23.) Which ones are not doing so well?

3. If you have a vegetable garden, think about ways of sharing its fruit. Instead of loading unwanted zucchini on your long-suffering neighbors, is there a food pantry that would be grateful for fresh garden produce?

4. How has gardening been a source of restoration for you? Write a short psalm of praise for the nourishment and healing God has given you.

5. The next time you plant, use this planting prayer:

   Creator God, Sovereign of the Universe, bless this seed/seedling with your gift of life. You make the soil, the seed, the sun, and the rain. And you made us as companions to you and your creation. May this seed/seedling grow, and may its beauty witness to your wonder and creativity. We praise and bless your name, God of the Universe. Amen.[13]

3 CONNECTING WITH CREATION

Awareness and Responsibility

The LORD God took the man and put him in
the garden of Eden to till it and keep it.
—Genesis 2:15

O LORD how manifold are your works!
  In wisdom you have made them all;
  the earth is full of your creatures.
—Psalm 104:24

The world is the bearer of the holy.
To destroy and degrade it violates God's
creative love.
—Henlee Barnette

All things by immortal power
near and far
hiddenly
to each other linked are.
Thou canst not stir a flower
without troubling a star.
—Francis Thompson

Several months ago, I clicked on my car radio and heard the end of a discussion on the recently published memoir of the biologist Edward O. Wilson. My attention was caught by the word *biophilia,* described as "affinity for the natural world." I was intrigued by the suggestion that this affinity is rooted deep within human nature. A few weeks later, *Modern Maturity* published an interview with Wilson in which he was asked, "Are there any other arguments for preserving species and biological diversity besides the ecological and economic ones?"

His answer was fascinating: "There are aesthetic arguments. You could even say they're spiritual. We have an affinity for the natural world. We cannot erase that evolutionary imprint in a few generations of urban living. Naturalists call this phenomenon *biophilia,* a term I first used in a book of essays by that title in 1984."[1] Wilson then went on to speak of the preference people have for natural scenes over urban ones, of the psychological benefits of having pets, of the love people have for the outdoors: backpacking, fishing, bird-watching, vacationing in the mountains or near water.

His comments struck a deep chord in me. I had experienced biophilia when I walked down a country lane at twilight: breathing in the calm, fresh air; rejoicing in the clear calls of six different birds and a chorus of crickets; marveling at the intricacy of the Queen Anne's lace festooning the roadside; observing two rabbits observing *me* with cautious eyes before they leap into the fresh-scented mountain mint growing under the pines. I found myself singing the words of a vespers hymn I learned as a child: "Heaven and earth are full of thee, heaven and earth are praising thee. . . ."

What I was feeling, and what Wilson identified for me, is a sense of connectedness to the garden of the Lord, the natural world. This idea is not a new one. The mystery of the bond between human creatures and the realm in which we live, that world "of rocks and trees, of skies and seas," of animals of infinite variety, is one about which poets have sung and philosophers have mused for thousands of years. This mystery has formed a part of many religions that have found something almost inexpressibly sacred in what we call nature. But the danger is that "nature" is sometimes substituted for "God." It is not enough to sit on a mountaintop and commune with nature. Our awe and wonder at the beauty and intricacy of the world around us should lead us instead to reflect on the magnificence of the Gardener who brought it into being, for creator and creation are indissolubly linked in biblical thought.

In the Old Testament, the word *nature* is never used for the world around us; nor is the word *creation*. In fact, there is no Hebrew word for nature. A form of the verb *bara* meaning "that which is being created" is used instead. Scripture always speaks of God's act of creating as ongoing and continuous, not completed; as dynamic, not static. Psalm 104 is a beautiful expression of this consciousness of God's ongoing activity in and care for the earth and its inhabitants.

The word *nature* itself comes from the Latin *natura,* meaning "that which is being born." In spite of this, however, we have lost that sense of the "ongoingness" of creation. Because we live in a technological society, where products roll off assembly lines as finished "creations," we transfer that image to the world around us and think of it as static and inert. We are just beginning to wake up to the importance of the biblical understanding. In his excellent book *We Are Home: A Spirituality of the Environment*, Shannon Jung, a theology professor at the University of Dubuque Theological Seminary, expresses his concern: "It is terribly illuminating that we have no trouble speaking of God as being active in history and culture, but much greater difficulty understanding God to be active in nature and continuing creation."[2]

When we use the word *creation* instead of the more ambiguous terms *nature* and *the cosmos,* we are affirming that there is indeed a Creator who "is the Ruler yet." In the early 1950s, I was deeply touched by Kurt Weill's musical *Lost in the Stars*, based on Alan Paton's classic novel about South Africa. In it, a poignant song, from which the title of the play is drawn, expresses the sense of despair felt by one of the characters enduring the horrors of the apartheid system. It is a song of abandonment, expressing the feeling that God may have created the world and then gone away, leaving us "lost out here in the stars."

The biblical affirmation is just the opposite: it affirms that the "earth is full of the steadfast love of the LORD" (Ps. 33:5). Over and over, in words like these, tribute is paid to the God who continues to care about creation:

> You visit the earth and water it,
>   you greatly enrich it;
> the river of God is full of water;

> you provide the people with grain,
> for so you have prepared it.
>   (Ps. 65:9)

Psalm 136 has a wonderful congregational response in each verse: "for his steadfast love endures forever." It is as if the composer of this hymn knew the woeful tendency of God's people to forget the enduring quality of God's sustaining care, not only for us but for all the created world. Many of us will never forget the black cover of a *Time* magazine issue in the 1970s, emblazoned with the red words "God Is Dead." The biblical testimony is that God is *not* dead but is a living, caring God, not a Gardener who goes on vacation and leaves the Garden to wither away but a Gardener who renews it and re-creates it with constancy and affection.

As a result of believing the world around us to be static and complete, we see it as separate and distinct from ourselves, thinking that it exists only to serve us. We believe that redemption is only for human souls. The biblical witness testifies otherwise—that we are redeemed *with* creation. Paul states it clearly:

> For the creation waits with eager longing for the revealing of the children of God . . . in hope that the creation itself will be set free from its bondage to decay and will obtain the freedom of the glory of the children of God. We know that the whole creation has been groaning in labor pains until now.
>   (Rom. 8:19, 21–22)

It is this link that is our real connection to creation, not "nature worship." The redemption of creation is not an easy idea for us to grasp. Will there be no more crabgrass or earthquakes or Japanese beetles or tornadoes? What about thorns and thistles? The idea was familiar in biblical times, however. The rabbis taught that although the created world was perfect in the beginning, it, too, was affected by the Fall, and that in the coming age, God will restore it to its Edenlike perfection. Isaiah 65:17 and Revelation 21:1 contain references not only to new heavens but to a new earth, a recognition that redemption not only is for spiritual realms but will affect the physical realm as well. Paul is saying that the created world will share in the redemption designed by God and will be set free "from the bondage to decay": no more tears, no more death, but glorious fullness and beauty.

MAKING CONNECTIONS

A recent article about Internet surfing said that 80 percent of all users are looking for "contact and commonality, companionship and community—all the conjugations implied by E. M. Forster's famous injunction, 'Only connect.'"[3]

Psalm 104 is about connecting—with the world around us and with its Creator. It is one of the most magnificent tributes to creation ever written. It begins by describing the wondrous power of the Creator, whose messengers are the winds and whose ministers are fire and flame, and how that Creator "set the earth on its foundations" (v. 5). The psalm paints a graphic picture of the loving care with which the Creator continues to irrigate and tend the earth until, as the psalmist says, "the earth is satisfied with the fruit of your work" (v. 13). As Calvin points out, "To make God a momentary Creator, who once for all finished his work, would be cold and barren. . . . He is also everlasting Governor and Preserver—not only in that he drives the celestial frame as well as its several parts by a universal motion, but also in that he sustains, nourishes, and cares for, everything he has made, even to the least sparrow."[4] This care is further illustrated in Psalm 104 by the provision God makes for how and where all creatures are to live: in fir trees, in high mountains, in rocks. The Creator "drives the celestial frame," as Calvin says, by determining the role of the sun and the moon, the length of the seasons and of days. The bottom line is that all living beings are dependent on the Creator, and all have their appointed tasks. For the psalmist who has recorded this stirring account of God's continuing care, the inevitable response is praise and admiration.

The psalmist has pictured for us a world in which there is a meaningful order, an overarching harmony; a world that exists solely because of the continuous care of its Creator and Sustainer. It is a psalm that calls us to recognize our connectedness with God and with all of God's creation. It reminds us of the importance of that creation and of all that is in it—rocks and trees, birds and wild goats, young lions and storks—for their own sakes, not because of their usefulness to human beings.

We connect with creation though attentiveness, awareness, and appreciation. It is so easy for us to take for granted our environment. It is especially easy for us to grow indifferent when our sojourns outdoors are limited to frenetic trips to amusement parks or lining up with thousands of other hot, tired tourists to see the Grand Canyon. We spend our days indoors, well insulated from the vagaries and beauties of nature by air-conditioning and shuttered windows.

It takes effort to be attentive. Thomas Berry, a monk who is one of the predominant "eco-theologians," writes, "What is needed on our part is the capacity for listening to what the earth is telling us."[5] I agree. While living in Africa, I discovered that my African friends seldom rhapsodized about "the beauty of nature," but they lived lives that were acutely attentive to it. They knew how to listen to the earth. Their dependence on the soil for sustenance made them sensitive to the best times for planting, to seasonal changes, to the location of edible forest plants. Their attentiveness made them aware of poisonous vegetation, of the ripening of the mangoes, or of the time to collect edible insects. Their appreciation was not for picture-postcard sunsets but for the coming of the rain across the hills and for good crops of manioc (cassava) and corn. My African friends never lost sight of the Gardener. Their close connection to the soil kept them connected to Nzambi, the Giver of Good Gifts.

It may not be important for us to know where the edible insects are, but we need desperately to become more attentive, more aware, and more appreciative of the world in which we live, in order to reestablish our sense of connectedness to it.

Two people who have spoken vividly about this need are Linda Filippi and Wendell Berry. Linda is the founder of a nonprofit organization in Albuquerque, New Mexico, whose purpose is to help people on limited incomes establish home vegetable gardens. In an interview, Linda said about her purpose in starting this organization:

> It is a radical act to garden. Most of our lives are mediated. Our food is grown somewhere else; we don't have much contact with the basic stuff of existence. To plant seeds is a radical act in the face of a culture that has disempowered us in so

many ways. We are afraid of being in deep relationship with each other . . . the earth . . . God. To plant a seed and begin that process is an act of hope.[6]

Wendell is a Kentucky farmer-poet who has written eloquently about the "fragmentation of Creation." He expresses the same concern as Linda:

> Only by restoring the broken connections can we be healed. Connection IS health. . . . We lose our health . . . by failing to see the direct connections between living and eating, eating and working, working and loving. In gardening, for instance, one works with the body to feed the body. The work, if it is knowledgeable, makes for excellent food. And it makes one hungry. The work thus makes eating both nourishing and joyful, not consumptive, and keeps the eater from getting fat and weak. This is health, wholeness, a source of delight.[7]

Both Linda Filippi and Wendell Berry see gardening as more than just a useful way to have fresh vegetables. They understand that something significant happens when we make contact with the "basic stuff of existence." We feel connected, a part of the wonderful, intricate system designed by God to sustain life on this planet. The very dirt beneath our fingernails is precious, a symbol of nourishment and richness.

TILLING AND CARING: STEWARDSHIP

The sense of separation from "the basic stuff of existence" described by Linda Filippi also existed in biblical times. After leaving Egypt, Israel wandered in the wilderness in search of a home, of roots, of land—of a "connectedness" with the earth. The people entered the land promised them by God with eager anticipation of settling in and putting down roots. But they discovered that "connectedness" brings with it an awareness of responsibility. As Walter Brueggemann has commented, "The same land which is gift freely given is task sharply put."[8]

It comes as a surprise to most of us to learn that many of the laws in Leviticus and Deuteronomy deal with land management. These laws were given to the people to spell out what it means to obey and honor God in concrete ways, in terms of the specifics of behavior toward others and toward the earth. One of those laws is largely forgotten today. We know about Sabbath rules that govern human behavior, even if we frequently disregard them. But a Sabbath for the land?

Leviticus is quite explicit:

> When you enter the land that I am giving you, the land shall observe a sabbath for the LORD. Six years you shall sow your field, and six years you shall prune your vineyard, and gather in their yield; but in the seventh year there shall be a sabbath of complete rest for the land, a sabbath for the LORD: you shall not sow your field or prune your vineyard. You shall not reap the aftergrowth of your harvest or gather the grapes of your unpruned vine: it shall be a year of complete rest for the land.
>
> (Lev. 25:2b–5)

The purpose of this law was to remind the people that God is the true owner of the land and has given the land to the people for their stewardship and care. In practical terms the law was a very good one, calling for crop rotation so that the fields could rest and renew themselves. In reality, however, farmers greedy for profit undid the benefits of the law by selling or trading off the land in the seventh, sabbatical year, so that the land never got a rest and eventually became a desert.

We don't hear much about a Sabbath for the land from our pulpits today, although crop rotation has proven to be a valuable practice in agriculture. I heard about a woman who decided to try this Sabbath concept in her own garden. Why not try it yourself? Prepare seven garden beds but take no harvest from one bed each year. In the unplanted bed, add mulch and compost and plant cover crops to be turned under to further enrich the soil. It's good agricultural wisdom, and it shows respect and reverence for the land.

Ecology has become a household word in the last twenty-five years. The tragic reason for our familiarity with this word is that we have so badly damaged the Garden into which God has placed us that panic has set in. On every side there are cries about global warming, the disappearance of the ozone layer, pollution of water and land, endangered animal species, the problem of nuclear-waste disposal, the impact of the loss of the rain forests on the rest of the world, the desertification of Africa. All of these are ecological problems. They are also *theological* problems.

A recognition of this has produced a growing emphasis on what is variously termed *environmental theology, eco-theology,* or a *theology of nature.* One of the clearest voices for this theology is that of Canadian theologian Douglas John Hall, who feels it is very important that we reinterpret the phrase "have dominion" to mean not "humanity above nature"—exercising mastery over it—but "humanity with nature"—servants, keepers, priests in relation to nature—which is the kind of "dominion" Jesus Christ demonstrated. "We are there to represent the others before their Maker and to represent to them—in our care of them—their Maker's care."[9] In similar fashion, theologian Sallie McFague of Vanderbilt Divinity School challenges us to "think of ourselves as gardeners, caretakers, mothers and fathers, stewards, trustees, lovers, priests, co-creators, and friends of a world that, while giving life and sustenance, also depends increasingly on us in order to continue both for itself and for us."[10]

In short, we are called to be stewards of God's creation, not owners of it. A steward in the biblical sense is a keeper, a caretaker, a custodian, whose first requirement is faithfulness. This is the true meaning of Gen. 2:15: "The Lord God took the man and put him in the garden of Eden to till it and keep it." The Garden that God planted needed a caretaker, an "apprentice gardener," so God gave this responsibility to human beings. The Hebrew word (*abad*) that is translated "till" or "work" means work in the sense of serving. Its companion word, *shamar,* usually translated "keep," means watchful care or preserving. We are called by God to serve the earth and to watch over it and preserve it. This is the true meaning of dominion.

We connect with the earth and its creatures through our serving and preserving them. We connect with God's creation when we recognize the interrelatedness of all creatures and their interdependence, when we celebrate the pleasure and sustenance the Garden gives us, and when we rejoice in the care and service we can give the Garden.

Christians have begun to be increasingly aware of their responsibility to provide that care and service to the Garden. In 1990 the 202nd General Assembly of the

Presbyterian Church (U.S.A.) issued a call to "respond to the cry of creation, human and nonhuman; to engage in the effort to make the 1990s the 'turnaround decade,' not only for reasons of prudence of survival, but because the endangered planet is God's creation; and to draw upon all the resources of biblical faith and the Reformed tradition for empowerment and guidance in this adventure." This call was based on the realization that "God's works in creation are too wonderful, too ancient, too beautiful, too good to be desecrated," and the conviction that "the Creator-Redeemer calls faithful people to become engaged with God in keeping and healing the creation, human and nonhuman."[11] We cannot ignore this call; our future, and our children's future, is at stake.

VISION OF SHALOM

When we speak of a harmonious relationship between human beings and the world around us, we are speaking in visionary terms. The reality, as we know, is quite different.

Henlee Barnette, author of *The Church and the Ecological Crisis*, points out the irony in the word *steward*. It comes from an Anglo-Saxon word meaning "keeper of a pig sty," and so Barnette warns:

> Remember that's what the prodigal son became when he wasted his inheritance. If the modern prodigal—the wasteful, spoiling polluter of the earth—continues to force nature to glorify himself instead of the Father in heaven, he may well find himself managing an environmental pig sty, and the original meaning of steward will be an ironically accurate description of his situation.[12]

The vision of harmony belongs to the future. We long for that time of reconciliation and harmony, of "paradise restored," that Isaiah described so beautifully in his picture of the peaceable kingdom. I have on the walls of my study sixty-five versions of this scene in which the wild beasts lie down with the animals of the fold. Several of them were painted by the Quaker artist Edward Hicks, whose imagination was so seized by Isaiah's words that he painted the scene at least eighty-three times. One ironic aspect of his paintings is that they nearly always include in the background the figure of William Penn, bargaining with Native Americans for the purchase of Pennsylvania, which for Hicks was to be the realization of the peaceable kingdom on earth.

In his description of the peaceable kingdom, Isaiah paints a picture of a return to the conditions of Eden, where wild beasts and dangerous reptiles live in harmonious companionship with domesticated animals and children (Isa. 11:6–8). The wolf lives with the lamb (not the lion; nowhere in the scripture does the "lion lie down with the lamb"), and the leopard lies down with the kid instead of tearing it apart. The phrase "lie down" literally means "become one of the flock." The lion, a natural predator, lies down with the calf and the fatling, two animals bred specifically to be sacrificed.

In these simple phrases we have a picture of a natural world turned upside down: those whose natural instinct is to kill no longer have to be predators; those to whose death society had consented no longer have to be victims. In the kingdom of God, as in the Garden of Eden, there are no oppressors, no oppressed. This "flock" of wild things and tame beasts is so docile it can be led by a little child.

This is the true meaning of shalom. We are not locked into destinies that cannot be changed. We are set free for the possibility of living in harmony with one another. When the lamb nuzzles up to the wolf, when the lion feeds peacefully with the calf and young bull, then human beings will also live together in peace and harmony, without having to kill and enslave and victimize one another and the world around them. There are no oppressors, no oppressed. This is the promise of the peaceable kingdom.

Shalom is more than just a vision of the ideal. It cries out for implementation in the here and now. As good stewards of the Garden of the Lord, we are to employ our minds and imaginations, our energies and ideas, to develop ways to make the peaceable kingdom a reality. Shalom is not just sweet peace among human beings. Shalom includes a recognition of our connectedness to and responsibility for the rest of God's creation as well. It calls us to a sacramental view of life and a renewed awareness of our stewarding tasks.

In April, Earth Day has been designated as a time for calling us to this renewed awareness of how to honor the earth. Why not include environmental awareness at other times in your church's life and worship? What about Thanksgiving, Stewardship Sunday, Lent, the first day of spring, and Easter as times to praise God for all of creation and to pray for that creation? You might ask your pastor to deliver a sermon on our responsibility for the earth. Use hymns that praise God's ongoing creative work in the world, such as "This Is My Father's World," "Come Sing with Joy to God," and "God, You Spin the Whirling Planets."

But even while we are doing all we can to be faithful in our stewardship, we are to remember the paradox: that true shalom is not accomplished entirely by the sweat of our brows but is a gift, a gift of the Gardener. It is God who works through us, who uses our hands to bring the vision to life, who teaches us how to garden. Our confidence and our hope rest in the fact that, as the old hymn suggests, the whole world is indeed in God's hands. Our God can preserve, protect, and defend the Garden without our help but honors us by inviting us to participate in its care as loving and thoughtful stewards.

PRAISING THE GARDENER

Creation is an invitation to wonder and to the praise of God. Not only in Psalm 104 but throughout the Psalms, the response to God's creative activity, especially in the world around us, is always praise, accompanied by deep humility: "Let all the earth fear the LORD; let all the inhabitants of the world stand in awe of him. For he spoke, and it came to be; he commanded, and it stood firm" (Ps. 33:8–9).

Psalm 8 carries the same theme:

> When I look at your heavens, the work of your fingers,
>   the moon and the stars that you have established;
> what are human beings that you are mindful of them,
>   mortals that you care for them?
>
> (Ps. 8:3–4)

The psalm is a hymn about the majesty and sovereignty of God, a majesty that is visible in creation. This is not pantheism, because there is a careful distinction between Creator and creation. Creation is an avenue to praise, not because it *is* God but because we begin to understand something of God's majesty as we experience the majesty of God's created works. In this hymn, the response of awe at God's majesty becomes an act of humility, of wonder that the sovereign God of the universe gives us both rights and responsibilities.

Praise is the response to the sense of connectedness we gain through awareness, attentiveness, and appreciation. It expresses itself in adoration. In an age when computers and television sets dazzle our eyes with explosions of color and sound, with images of faraway places, with glimpses inside cells and across galaxies, we so easily become blasé. We lose our ability to be amazed. We are no longer filled with awe at midnight skies and grasshopper legs. If we are to experience in a vivid way our connectedness to the Garden of the Lord, we must reclaim "the four a's" and let resounding songs of adoration of God be the end result of our awareness, attentiveness, and appreciation of God's Garden.

The rabbinic tradition of Israel recounts a tale about the creation of the world. Having completed everything in five days, the Creator asked one of the attending angels whether anything was still missing. The angel answered that everything was, of course, perfect, as one might expect of God's handiwork. "Yet perhaps," the angel ventured, "perhaps one thing could make this already perfect work yet more perfect: speech, to praise its perfection." God thereupon approved the angel's words and created the human creature.[13]

A FINAL WORD

We are given a Garden to live in, planted by the Good Gardener. That Gardener wants us to connect with that Garden through attentiveness, awareness, and appreciation. As we do so, our ecological concerns become theological ones, as we realize that our sense of harmony with all of creation gives us a glimpse of the true meaning of shalom. Our natural, inevitable response to the Gardener is wonder, awe, humility, and heartfelt praise.

FOR SPIRITUAL GROWTH

1. Take a "connecting" walk. Be aware, attentive, and appreciative. Notice the variety of wildflowers, the shapes of leaves. Count the birdcalls you hear. Hug a tree. (India's "Embrace a Tree" movement was an intentional effort to revive respect for trees in a land where forests were rapidly becoming denuded for firewood.) Write a prayer of praise to God for the ongoing creation around us. Include in it a petition for forgiveness for our part in the careless destruction of the Garden that God has given us.

2. Go on a field trip. Take a tour of your town's garbage dump, water supply, sewage treatment plant, recycling center, power plant, nuclear-waste site, and so forth. Learn more about what happens to the waste your community produces. Prepare questions ahead of time to ask the person who shows you or your group around. Follow up by writing a report for your church newsletter or your community newspaper, to share the information you have gained.

3. Change your lifestyle to help save the planet! Here are some things you can do.

   Use cloths instead of paper towels to wipe up spills.
   Use cold water to wash clothes.
   Alternate use of cloth and disposable diapers.
   Start a compost pile.
   Take plastic pots back to the nursery.
   Return coat hangers to the cleaners.
   Use reusable shopping bags instead of plastic ones.
   Ride a bike or walk for short trips.
   Avoid Styrofoam.
   And *don't litter!*[14]

4 LIKE A WATERED GARDEN

Healing and Renewal

The LORD will open for you his rich storehouse, the heavens, to give the rain of your land in its season and to bless all your undertakings.

—Deuteronomy 28:12

The LORD will guide you continually,
    and satisfy your needs in parched places,
    and make your bones strong;
and you shall be like a watered garden,
    like a spring of water,
    whose waters never fail.

—Isaiah 58:11

Lovely! See the cloud, the cloud appear!
Lovely! See the rain, the rain draw near!
            —Zuni corn-grinding song

When the well's dry, we know the worth of water.
                —Benjamin Franklin

Great wide, beautiful, wonderful world,
With the wonderful water round you curled,
And the wonderful grass upon your breast,
World, you are beautifully dressed.
            —William Brighty Rands

Water is life.

We gardeners know what happens when newly planted seeds or seedlings do not get enough water. The parsley won't sprout, the squash leaves turn yellow, the tomatoes split, the beans dry up. And then the clouds darken, the thunder rumbles, and the heavens release the precious gift of rain. We see with our own eyes how that gift brings life to dry, inert soil and restores and refreshes our limp and wilted plants. If rainfall is short, we pore over gardening catalogs for equipment that will make the task of supplying water easier: oscillating sprinklers, perforated hoses, watering tubes, watering cans for hard-to-reach places. Water is not an option for gardens; it is a must.

In the Bible, references to the importance of water for garden life begin in Genesis. Even before the rains began, an underground stream rose up to "water the whole face of the ground" (Gen. 2:6), in preparation for the plants and herbs of the field. This story reminds us that life itself is the gift of God. It is God who provides the water that brings life to the dust of the earth and greens its barren rocks with plants and herbs. It is God who causes the rain to fall, to keep those plants and herbs fresh and growing.

After God planted the garden, a river with four branches watered it. Ezekiel and John mention these river branches in their visions of a new paradise. On the banks of these rivers grow trees whose healing leaves never wither and which bear constant fruit, because water for them flows from the very throne of God (Ezek. 47:12; Rev. 22:1–2).

It was this image of a green, lush garden watered by underground springs and coursing rivers that was in Lot's mind when he was offered his choice of land by Abraham as they came up from Egypt into Palestine: "Lot looked about him, and saw that the plain of the Jordan was well watered everywhere like the garden of the Lord, like the land of Egypt. . . . So Lot chose for himself all the plain of the Jordan" (Gen. 13:10–11a). Water was a crucial element in Lot's decision, because no village or city could be built without a good water supply.

Water was and is very precious in the Middle East. The climate has changed little since biblical times. Many areas of Palestine have almost no rainfall. At

Jerusalem the average rainfall is twenty-two inches a year, but at Jericho, only two. In the extreme south, rainfall is too sparse to support permanent farming. The hill country has the highest rainfall, and both rainfall and soil fertility decrease from north to south. In biblical times, the levels of rainfall in different areas divided the country into wheat land and barley land, because barley takes less rain.

Now, as then, the uncertainty of the time of the rains and the amount of rainfall make rain the most important element of the climate. The amount of rainfall has always varied from year to year, and a drop in precipitation of an inch or two below the average can mean disaster for crops. Generally, the first rains have begun in October and lasted until the hot, dry summer starts in May. This pattern of drought from May to September was one to which farmers in ancient times learned to adapt. More devastating for them than drought were the occasional very early rains, followed by another dry period, which caused seeds to sprout, then die for lack of water. Problems were also caused by a delay in the rains, especially in the Negev, where the vegetation actually burns off from the ferocity of the sun if the rains are late.

The Negev, the country south of Hebron that extended from Beersheba on the north to Kadesh on the south, was one of the driest areas in biblical times, although it was not as barren a desert as it is today. As Abraham went to and fro from Egypt, he was able to find pastures and water for his numerous cattle (Gen. 12:9–13:1). Later, during the patriarchal period, the wells and pasture lands disappeared, perhaps because of tribal wars, and the land was dry. Even today, when sudden rains do appear in this area, there is a swift and dramatic change. In just an hour or so the deep ravines, called wadis, can fill with water and cause flash floods. The psalmist uses this familiar image of sudden change in a plea to God to reverse the fortunes of Zion, so it will have new life "like the watercourses in the Negeb" (Ps. 126:4).

The need to farm these arid lands led to the development of terrace agriculture, fed by runoff water from the flash floods. King Uzziah seems to have had a personal interest in agriculture and to have been particularly concerned about provision of water in the Negev. He had great cisterns hewn out of stone, to water cattle. But it was the Nabateans (who occupied this area after the fall of Judah) who demonstrated the greatest skill in practicing water conservation, building dams, cisterns, and more terraces to hold the precious water. During New Testament times, the Negev was once again a place for farming as well as raising cattle.[1]

Throughout the history of Palestine, desert nomads have searched eagerly in the desert for oases with their precious springs. A major source of these springs was the melting snow from the high mountains of Lebanon and Mount Hermon in the north. This water sank into the ground and later emerged as springs in the desert. The snows were also the source of the Sea of Galilee and the Jordan River.

The early settlers of Palestine learned how to supplement these natural sources of water with wells that tapped into underground streams. "Jacob's well" in Samaria, where Jesus encountered the Samaritan woman (John 4), was one of these. It was over one hundred feet deep and about eight feet in diameter and was covered by a large stone with a chiseled hole in the center. Women drew water through this hole using ropes and leather buckets that they brought with them. A stranger without a bucket (like Jesus in the Samaritan woman story) had no access to the water and had to rely on the kindness of others. Although this well is never mentioned in the Old Testament, the tradition is that the well had been given by Jacob for the Israelites and their flocks to use. Even in Jesus' day, this well had never been known to go dry and had become revered as a symbol for God's sustaining care and life-giving power.

People also relied on cisterns to catch and hold rainwater. Most homes had their own cisterns, but communal underground reservoirs also served the towns and cities. If these should become dry from delayed rains or if the cistern became cracked (see Jer. 2:13), people would be desperate for water. At such times, water was sold in the street by measure.

Given the importance of water in this dry land, it is not surprising that it became a central metaphor in biblical poetry, sermons, proverbs, curses, and blessings. There are over a hundred mentions in scripture of drought and the famine that accompanied it. Because drought was clearly the most feared disaster, because people's very lives hung on the amount of rain that fell on their crops, water was a powerful symbol of God's blessing, of spiritual refreshment, of hope, of growth, and of life.

WATER AS A BLESSING FROM GOD

In the Sango language of the Central African Republic, the word for rain literally means "God-water." The Israelites felt much the same way about this blessing. An assurance of rain was an important part of God's covenant promise to them:

> But the land that you are crossing over to occupy is a land of hills and valleys, watered by rain from the sky, a land that the LORD your God looks after. . . . He will give the rain for your land in its season, the early rain and the later rain, and you will gather in your grain, your wine, and your oil; and he will give grass in your fields for your livestock, and you will eat your fill.
>
> (Deut. 11:11–12a, 14–15)

The inclusion of this promise in the covenant was a constant reminder to the Israelites of their dependence on God, because it is God who provides the rain that made it possible for them to gather in grain, wine, and oil.

The covenant promises about rain also contain warnings. If the people turned away from the Lord to worship other gods, the result would be that "there will be no rain and the land will yield no fruit" (Deut. 11:17). Solomon begged God to forgive the Israelites and grant them rain when they repented of the sins that had brought on a drought (see 1 Kings 8:35–36). Warnings about drought occur frequently in the words of the prophets. For example, in Isaiah's first Song of the Vineyard (Isa. 5:1–7), a part of the punishment is that the clouds will rain no rain on the vineyard that represents Israel, God's "pleasant planting." And Jeremiah saw Judah's sin as so great that even after God sent a drought as punishment, she still had not abandoned her harlotry (Jer. 3:3). He described the devastation of that drought:

> They are ashamed and dismayed
>   and cover their heads,
> because the ground is cracked.
>   Because there has been no rain on the land
> the farmers are dismayed;
>   they cover their heads.
>
> (Jer. 14:3b–4)

Even though the people begged God to deliver them from the drought, Jeremiah realized that their repentance was shallow: they remembered God when times were hard; they forgot God when things were going well. They were a people who "loved to wander," and because of this, they would be punished by not receiving the blessing of rain.

Again and again in scripture, the provision of rain is an indication of God's love and care. The purpose of Elijah's contest on Mount Carmel with the prophets of the Canaanite (Phoenician) god Baal (1 Kings 18:20–40) was to demonstrate forcibly to the people that it is the Lord God, not Baal, who controls the rain. Job's friends Eliphaz and Elihu describe God to Job as the sovereign ruler of nature and use the giving of rain as an example of God's power (Job 4:10; 36:27–28). The psalmists extolled God as the one who makes the earth fertile and blesses it with rain:

> You visit the earth and water it,
>   you greatly enrich it;
> the river of God is full of water;
>   you provide the people with grain,
>   for so you have prepared it.
> You water its furrows abundantly,
>   settling its ridges,
> softening it with showers,
>   and blessing its growth.
>   (Ps. 65:9–10)

The prophets also, in calling the people to obedience and loyalty, used the symbol of rain as a reminder of why they should be grateful to God and uphold their part of the covenant. Isaiah promises that God will give rain for seed and brooks running with water (Isa. 30:23, 25). Zechariah echoes this theme:

> Ask rain from the LORD
>   in the season of the spring rain,
> from the LORD who makes the storm clouds,

who gives showers of rain to you,
the vegetation in the field to everyone.
(Zech. 10:1)

Even the dew was considered a blessing from God. Isaac's blessing of Jacob contains these words: "May God give you the dew of heaven, and of the fatness of the earth, and plenty of grain and wine" (Gen. 27:28). Esau, who should have been the recipient of this blessing, received instead a meager "blessing" that denied him the "fatness of the earth" and the "dew of heaven" but did promise him and his descendants eventual freedom from Jacob. Isaac did what he could for his beloved son who had been tricked, but Esau nonetheless hated Jacob because of the deceit that deprived him of his agricultural heritage. Esau's descendants, living in the dry, arid land of Edom, where both dew and rain were indeed scarce, perpetuated this hatred of the Israelites.

In the New Testament, when Paul and Barnabas were hailed as gods by the people of Lystra, they hastened to correct that impression by speaking of "the living God, who . . . has not left himself without a witness in doing good—giving you rains from heaven and fruitful seasons, and filling you with food and your hearts with joy" (Acts 14:15, 17). The two were trying to point the Lystrans to God by reminding them of the blessings of everyday life: rain, fruitful crops, food, and joyfulness—all of which are the gifts of God.

People who live close to the land are quick to make the connection between rain and the blessing of God. A prayer from Africa expresses this association:

Rejoice in the Lord,
for he has caused the parched earth to be refreshed,
and where there was nothing but brownness, hardness and
death, there is now greenness covering the soft earth.
Where there was death there is now newness of life, hope has been restored
throughout the land.[2]

Those of us who live in highly technological societies, however, frequently lose this sense of dependence on God for rain. The miracle of faucet water, to say nothing of city reservoirs, rural water systems, highly complicated machines for sprinkling and irrigating crops—all insulate us from the reality of the Gardener's role in the gift of water. We take for granted that the county or the city will supply us with water and forget to respond in gratitude to the True Giver. But like the lives of people in biblical times, our lives are dependent on this blessing from God. Every time we drink a glass of water or take a shower or turn on a hose, we should give thanks to the one who says, "I give water in the wilderness, rivers in the desert, to give drink to my chosen people, the people whom I formed for myself so that they might declare my praise" (Isa. 43:20–21).

WATER AS A SYMBOL FOR SPIRITUAL REFRESHMENT

In addition to using the physical gift of water as a sign of God's blessing and loving care, the Bible speaks of water in metaphorical way: a symbol for life, renewal, and spiritual refreshment. The water of God will make Isaiah's prophecy come true: "The wilderness and the dry land shall be glad, the desert shall rejoice and blossom; like the crocus it shall blossom abundantly, and rejoice with joy and singing. . . . Waters shall break forth in the wilderness, and streams in the desert; the burning sand shall become a pool, and the thirsty ground springs of water; the haunt of jackals shall become a swamp, the grass shall become reeds and rushes" (Isa. 35:1–2, 6–7).

Spiritual drought is a not uncommon experience for even the most devout Christians. Prayer lives dry up; interest in spiritual things droops like unwatered plants. Life, love, and hope seem meaningless. In such times, it is comforting to know that even "spiritual giants" such as John of the Cross, C. S. Lewis, Thomas Merton, and Martin Marty have experienced the same dryness and have written honestly about it. In her devotional classic *Revelation of Divine Love,* written in the 1300s, Julian of Norwich suggested that in times of spiritual drought, Christ wishes us to "pray inwardly, even though you find no joy in it. For it does good, though you feel nothing, see nothing, yes, even though you think you cannot pray. For when you are dry and empty, sick and weak, your prayers please me, though there be little enough to please you. All believing prayer is precious to me."[3]

We can learn, perhaps, from the respected contemporary writer on spirituality Richard Foster, who describes his own times of dryness in this way: "Have you ever tried to pray and felt nothing, saw nothing, sensed nothing? Has it ever seemed like your prayers did no more than bounce off the ceiling and ricochet around an empty room?" The solution he suggests is much like the one given by Julian: "To ask and continue to ask even though there is no answer. . . . While the wilderness is necessary, it is never meant to be permanent. In God's time and in God's way the desert will give way to a land flowing with milk and honey."[4]

Foster's image of the desert as a symbol of spiritual drought is similar to Isaiah's beautiful words in chapter 58, where the "parched places" are contrasted with a "watered garden." For Isaiah, water is a symbol for God's gift of guidance and replenishment in the desert times of life:

> The LORD will guide you continually,
>   and satisfy your needs in parched places,
>   and make your bones strong;
> and you shall be like a watered garden,
>   like a spring of water,
>   whose waters never fail.
>
> (Isa. 58:11)

It is likely that the prophet was drawing on the image of an oasis: a welcome sight to travelers "in parched places," moving through scorching desert heat. These words are a reminder that God's waters do not dry up but are capable of bringing us to life no matter how dry we are.

Like Isaiah, Psalm 23 also speaks of God's guidance and care, leading us "beside still waters," and supplying all our needs so that we "shall not want." These words have provided comfort to thousands of people. The peaceful imagery of green pastures and still waters is one not only of security and safety but of being cared for with refreshment and nourishment. Many people who lead stressed-out lives in the concrete jungles of cities feel a deep need to get away to greenness and water, to lakes, rivers, and seashores. They speak of a "restoration of the soul" that comes to them from being near water.

But Isaiah 58 is speaking of more than just physical and psychological renewal. He is speaking of the "water of life," the miracle of God's grace that goes abundantly above all that we can ask or think to make our parched lives "like watered gardens." Shakespeare spoke of mercy as dropping like "gentle rain from heaven." It is that gentle rain of God's mercy, the miraculous fountain of God's forgiveness, and the deep well of God's steadfast love that bring us out of our despair, our emptiness, our meaninglessness, our hopelessness, and that make our gardens live again.

To benefit from this life-giving water, we must be ready. As we have already seen, hard-packed garden soil is unable to receive the spring rains. Our soil must be made ready in repentance and openness, in hope and trust. Hosea understood this when he wrote, "Break up your fallow ground; for it is time to seek the LORD, that he may come and rain righteousness upon you" (Hos. 10:12). The Gardener is ready; the rains will come, and our "parched places" will become green and alive again.

WATER AS A SIGN OF HOPE

Jeremiah 31:2–40 is a beautiful passage that has been referred to as the "Little Book of Consolation." It spells out in the clearest possible terms the certainty of Israel's hope, grounded in the message of salvation. It was a message that the scattered remnant in exile desperately needed to hear. Even though they sat down by the rivers of Babylon, those streams and canals of the Tigris and Euphrates rivers did not quench their thirst. Just as David longed for water from the familiar well at Bethlehem when he was a fugitive (2 Sam. 23:15), saying, "O that someone would give me water to drink from the well of Bethlehem that is by the gate!" the children of Israel in exile longed for the familiar waters of their homeland.

Jeremiah's message is powerful. He reminds Israel that its hope comes from God's everlasting love and faithfulness, that the one who made them will not abandon them but will "let them walk by brooks of water" (31:9). To emphasize this love, he adds these words:

> For the LORD has ransomed Jacob,
>   and has redeemed him from hands too strong for him.

> They shall come and sing aloud on the height of Zion,
>   and they shall be radiant over the goodness of the LORD,
> over the grain, the wine, and the oil,
>   and over the young of the flock and the herd;
> their life shall become like a watered garden,
>   and they shall never languish again.
>
> (Jer. 31:11–12)

This image, so much like the one in Isaiah 58, describes a time of renewed prosperity and happiness, a coming home of scattered people. It is an exuberant family reunion, a thanksgiving feast where everyone's face glows with gratitude and joy for the blessings from God. As Jeremiah searched for words to picture the beautiful hope of restoration and fullness that God was offering Israel, he decided on the image of a watered garden, a perpetual oasis, a place where all needs would be satisfied and they would "never languish again."

The word *languish* is an interesting one. It carries with it the connotations of prolonged suffering, lack of energy and vitality, and general lifelessness caused by discouraging situations. Most of us have languished at some time. Physical illness can cause this, or depression that deprives us of energy and enthusiasm. It may be the result of boredom or apathy, the feeling that all the juice has been sucked out of life and nothing matters any more. We "languish" when we feel battered and bruised by life, when so much has gone wrong that hope for a better life seems very dim and far away. In extreme cases, this may result in the despair of "There's nothing worth living for!"

Many have experienced the languishing of loneliness, the feeling that no one knows or cares that we exist, not even God. The pain of loneliness is a frequent theme in the lament psalms. In Psalm 102 the psalmist cries out, "I lie awake; I am like a lonely bird on the housetop" (Ps. 102:7). What Jeremiah is saying is that even in our darkest hours we must not give up hope, for we are not alone. The Gardener has not forsaken us but, even when we are drooping like unwatered tomato plants on a hot summer day, will be there to provide those showers of blessing we need. Hosea speaks of these showers poignantly:

> Let us know, let us press on to know the LORD;
>> his appearing is as sure as the dawn;
> he will come to us like the showers,
>> like the spring rains that water the earth.
>>>> (Hos. 6:3)

In the New Testament, James uses the hope for rain as a symbol of encouragement for Christians experiencing hardships and difficulties in practicing their faith:

> Be patient, therefore, beloved, until the coming of the Lord. The farmer waits for the precious crop from the earth, being patient with it until it receives the early and the late rains. You must also be patient. Strengthen your hearts, for the coming of the Lord is near.
>
>>>> (James 5:7–8)

James's message is important for us to hear. Each time we pray, "Thy kingdom come," we are making an affirmation of hope. We are saying that we do indeed believe that our times are in God's hands and that the future belongs to God. This hope is not for "pie in the sky, by and by," but is a statement of trust in God's plan. We are called to be patient but not passive. We are to "strengthen our hearts"; to live as the farmer lives, going about our tasks simply and faithfully, trusting patiently in God's loving care, and believing that God has a redemptive purpose for the world. Both memory (of God's loving acts in the past) and hope (of God's promises of what is to come) sustain us in painful desert experiences.

WATER AS NECESSARY FOR GROWTH

The Bible recognizes the reality of spiritual thirst as well as physical thirst. Water was used often in scripture as a symbol for spiritual renewal and growth. In Job, Bildad the Shuhite asks the question "Can papyrus grow where there is no marsh? Can reeds flourish where there is no water?" (Job 8:11). He is using these unwatered plants as a metaphor for the godless, who will "wither before any other plant." Jeremiah contrasted the fruitlessness of the "shrub in the desert," which lives in the "parched places of the wilderness," with the "tree planted by water, sending out its roots by the stream" (Jer. 17:6, 8). This tree does not fear the heat and drought but always has green leaves and plenty of fruit. It is likely that Jeremiah was speaking of the olive tree, which is an exceptionally hardy tree in Palestine but which dies without water. In fact, olives do best when planted by a river or by the sea, where the mists keep them constantly moist.

The passage in which these verses are found (Jer. 17:5–10) reflects the style of wisdom literature in its contrast of those who trust in human knowledge and wisdom and "make mere flesh their strength" and those "whose trust is the Lord." Jeremiah goes deeper than the traditional wisdom approach, however, in suggesting that it is this very trust in God that gives life, that makes the righteous person "stay green." This contrast between the person who is alienated from God, trusting in abundant riches instead, and the one who finds joy and meaning in the steadfast love of God also finds expression in Ps. 52:8:

> But I am like a green olive tree
>   in the house of God.
> I trust in the steadfast love of God
>   forever and ever.

Jeremiah's words are also very much like Psalm 1 in the contrast between the way of the wicked and the way of the righteous. Psalm 1 describes righteous persons as being "like trees planted by streams of water, which yield their fruit in its season, and their leaves do not wither" (Ps. 1:3). These righteous persons seek to know the meaning and value of life by focusing on God's word and living in obedience to God. They are renewed by the life-giving power of the word, just as the tree is renewed by the life-giving power of the water it receives from the streams.

As Christians, we value spiritual growth, but most of us are still in process in our spiritual journeys. We are all thirsty for more, recognizing that the growth of our spiritual gardens is a process that is never finished. Maya Angelou spoke wisely when she said in a television interview, "I'm trying to be a Christian and it's not an easy thing to do. When people walk up to me and say, 'I'm a Christian,' I say, 'Already?'"

Throughout scripture, the spiritually alive person is pictured as a growing person. One example is in 1 Peter: "Like newborn infants, long for the pure, spiritual milk, so that by it you may grow into salvation—if indeed you have tasted that the Lord is good" (1 Peter 2:2). This kind of growth demands humility. The kind of arrogant attitude that assumes it already has all the answers stifles growth. A growing person is an eager person with a thirst that must be assuaged, like the "ground that drinks up the rain falling on it repeatedly" (Heb. 6:7). The growing person has the attitude of the servant, who says of God, "Every morning he makes me eager to hear what he is going to teach me" (Isa. 50:4, TEV).

Inevitably, growth means change. Every gardener knows that a growing garden is different from day to day, from season to season, from seedtime to harvest. A part of the fun for gardeners is inspecting the garden to see what new surprises of growth have occurred. Are the cucumbers blossoming? Have the eggplants begun to set fruit? Are the tomatoes ripe yet? If a garden becomes static, if nothing is changing, then growth has stopped and it is dead.

Some years ago, I wrote a ballad of affirmation of growth:

On a hill an olive tree,
Sank its roots into the ground.
And the winds blew
But it stood firm,
For those roots were long and sound.

That old tree has stood for years
And its limbs are bent, it's true.
But it's still young,
For it still grows
And each year its leaves are new.

REFRAIN:
I am like that olive tree,
Always changing,

Still a-greening,
Blown by winds but
Young and strong.

The "water of life" keeps us "always changing, still a-greening," so that we may remain "young and strong" in the practice of our faith.

WATER AS A PROMISE OF LIFE

This chapter began with the words "Water is life." Again and again, in both the Old and New Testaments, writers seized on this image as a way to give shape and definition to the essential truth of existence: that just as our physical selves cannot live without water, our spiritual selves shrivel up and die apart from the life-giving fountain of God's love.

Isaiah issued an invitation to all who are not satisfied with the emptiness and dryness of their lives, with "labor that does not satisfy": "Ho, everyone who thirsts, come to the waters; . . . listen, so that you may live" (Isa. 55:1, 3). This invitation is very similar to the banquet invitation given by Wisdom in Proverbs 9: "Come, eat my bread and drink of the wine I have mixed. . . . For by me your days will be multiplied, and years will be added to your life" (Prov. 9:5, 11). It is more likely, however, that Isaiah modeled his invitation on the cries of water sellers advertising their wares in the public market during times of drought. Unlike the sellers, though, God is offering the kind of water that does not just quench physical thirst but that brings life in its fullness to those suffering spiritual drought. It is a message of salvation, healing, renewal; of the wondrous possibilities of a new life, a life with God.

It is possible that Jesus had Isaiah 55 in mind when he told the Samaritan woman, "Those who drink of the water that I will give them will never be thirsty" (John 4:14). Earlier, Jesus had spoken of *living water*, a term used to distinguish the rushing water of a stream or river from the placid water of the well to which the woman had come. What did Jesus mean by "living water"? Not himself, suggests New Testament scholar Raymond Brown, but something that can lead to eternal life. Brown believes that this allows for two possibilities: living water may be either

Jesus' teaching or the Spirit communicated by Jesus.[5] If Jesus was referring to eternal life that comes from heeding his teachings, he may have had in mind passages from the Old Testament where water is a symbol of God's life-giving wisdom: "The teaching of the wise is a fountain of life" (Prov. 13:14); "The fountain of wisdom is a gushing stream" (Prov. 18:4). If he is referring to the gift of the Spirit, he may be influenced by other passages that make a connection between water and spirit, such as "I will pour water on the thirsty land, and streams on the dry ground; I will pour my spirit upon your descendants, and my blessing on your offspring" (Isa. 44:3).

Perhaps the truth is that Jesus' use of this wonderful metaphor included both ideas, for the abundant life (John 10:10) of which he is speaking is revealed to us both in his teachings and through the work of the Holy Spirit, who interprets those teachings. Both of these form the "springs of water" that are the source of greening into newness.

Carolyn Huffman writes about her experience of the Spirit as living water in her wonderful book, *Meditations on a Rose Garden*:

> In my own life, I have found that the Holy Spirit, God's living water, can and will bless others through me. If I try to hold this blessing only for myself, then I, like rosebushes with poor drainage, become static and stale, and sometimes I drown. If I compromise the conduit, take shortcuts in my daily relationship with God, then just a trickle of God's blessing can flow where it is supposed to go. Knowingly and unknowingly, I often am careless about keeping the conduits of God's loving presence repaired; consequently, some of God's blessings can never blossom in my life—or in the lives of those around me.[6]

Nowhere in Christian tradition is water more clearly a symbol of new life than in the sacrament of baptism. Early in the history of the church, new Christians were baptized just outside the church or at the entrance to the sanctuary. Baptism symbolized being washed clean of sin and the beginning of new life in Christ, as well as becoming part of a new community of faith. This new life was the result of the "living water," the gift of God's grace in Jesus Christ and Holy Spirit, to which believers have responded and to which they will continue to respond each day for the rest of their lives. Just as the spring rains cause seeds to spring to new life, the water of baptism reminds us of the grace that brings us to life so that our gardens, too, may bear rich fruit.

A FINAL WORD

Water: a blessing from God, a symbol for spiritual refreshment, a sign of hope, a reminder of the grace of God that keeps us alive and growing.

Water: a metaphor for the revelation of God through Jesus Christ and the Holy Spirit, which makes possible a rich, abundant, fruitful life.

Water: the gift of the loving Gardener, who not only plants us but keeps us alive with showers of blessings that bring us back to life when we are parched and dry.

FOR SPIRITUAL GROWTH

1. Pour a cup of water and give it your full attention. Take a sip. Let it trickle slowly down your throat, feeling its liquid coolness. Dip your fingers into the cup and splash water on your forehead, neck, and arms. Think about a time when you were very thirsty and someone gave you water. Now, drink the water slowly, savoring each mouthful. Write a prayer of thanksgiving and praise for the gift of water.

2. Take a walk in the rain. Notice the sights and sounds around you as the rain splashes on leaves and flowers, on pavement and in the dust. Let it fall onto your face; feel its refreshing coolness. And if you feel like it, do a little "singin' in the rain!"

3. Have you ever experienced spiritual dryness? In what ways did you receive refreshment and renewal—from a friend, from a book, through prayer or scripture, in a time of retreat and meditation?

4. Read about the destruction of the tropical rainforests and how this problem is affecting climate and agriculture all over the world. Most of us have never seen a rainforest, so we have trouble understanding how this problem could affect us. But this has become a serious problem for the world community. Get in touch with The Rainforest Action Network, 301 Broadway, Suite A, San Francisco, California 94133, to find out what you can do about the issue.[7]

5 WEEDING AND PRUNING

Discipline and Confrontation

Thorns and snares are in the way of the perverse;
  the cautious will keep far from them.
                              —Proverbs 22:5

Life is thorny.
  —Coleridge

A man of words and not of deeds
Is like a garden full of weeds.
                              —Anonymous

Now 'tis the spring, and weeds are shallow-rooted;
Suffer them now and they'll overgrow the garden.
                              —Shakespeare

Every branch that bears fruit he prunes to make it bear more fruit.
                              —John 15:2

God is a zealous pruner,
For He knows—

> Who, falsely tender, spares the knife
> But spoils the rose.
>   —John Oxenham, 1852–1941

I really don't like weeds. Emerson may be right that a weed is "a plant whose virtues have not yet been discovered," but this attitude of philosophical tolerance doesn't help me much when I find grass invading my herb beds and marching on the zucchini. In the South, one of the most awe-inspiring "weeds" is kudzu, a large-leafed vine that covers tall trees, abandoned school buses, even houses. It turns them into weird shapes that look like green versions of the famous rounded limestone pinnacles along the Li River in China. Kudzu is beautiful, but deadly for the trees and bushes it smothers.

Weeds are not welcome in my garden patch because they refuse to live side by side, in orderly amity, with other garden plants. They want it all: all the space, all the soil, all the water, all the nutrients. And my meek, well-bred little vegetable seedlings give up without much of a fight when choked out by these aggressive opponents.

Briers are even worse, for they add to "weed greediness" a purely vicious streak. If you try to disentangle them from the nandinas, they fight back—and even draw blood. And as for other pricklies, rose growers and cactus lovers sometimes pay dearly for the care they give their thorny, spiny plants.

It's not a new problem. Three thousand years ago, as the land of Palestine became well cultivated, as fields and orchards were laid out, irrigated, and tended, the enemy was there. Thorns, nettles, brambles, thistles, darnel (the ominous weed of Matthew 13), and other weeds made the farmer's life difficult. Proverbs sets forth a vivid description of what happens to lazy gardeners:

> I passed by the field of one who was lazy,
>   by the vineyard of a stupid person;
> and see, it was all overgrown with thorns;

the ground was covered with nettles,
and its stone wall was broken down.
                              (Prov. 24:30, 31)

THORNS, NETTLES, AND THISTLES: SYMBOLS OF HARDSHIP AND DISASTER

Many types of thorny plants are mentioned in scripture. At least twenty Hebrew words are used to indicate prickly plants, but no clear distinction is made among thorns, briers, brambles, and thistles. Various types of thornbushes form an abundant part of the landscape of Palestine. They are commonly used as hedges to separate fields and encircle vineyards. In biblical times they were extensively used as fuel for kilns and ovens, and in some areas this is still the practice. It is common in the Middle East to see donkeys piled so high with dried thornbushes that the animals are barely visible as they trudge along. One will see the piles of thorns and briers, ready for burning, beside black goat-hair tents. In biblical times, when used as firewood, the thorns were gathered and cut up with pruning hooks. The author of Ecclesiastes refers to use of thorns as fuel in making a caustic comparison between "the crackling of thorns under a pot" and "the laughter of fools" (Eccl. 7:6).

In Jotham's ironic satire on the monarchy, the parable of the trees (Judg. 9:8–15), the bramble is selected as ruler over the trees when the olive, fig, and vine refuse the position. The bramble was perhaps a type of blackberry and appears in this parable as a symbol of worthlessness, since, unlike the others, it did not produce rich oil, delicious fruit, and "wine that cheers gods and mortals" (Judg. 9:13) but was good only to be burned up as fuel.

Closely related to thorns are nettles and thistles. The stinging nettle grows in unweeded gardens and uncultivated fields. It must have grown to enormous size, for Job describes how the outcasts who mock him "huddle together" under the nettles (Job 30:7). The star thistle thrives in every part of Palestine today.

The curse in Gen. 3:17–19 of "thorns and thistles" does not seem an enormous tragedy today, but it paints a graphic picture of the difference between "joyous work" and "painful toil." It is a reminder that life outside the garden is filled with pain and sweat and stings. Thornless roses and blackberries, noninvasive weeds, and honeysuckle-free hedges grow only in Eden: another vision of the shalom that will ultimately be "God's kingdom on earth."

Isaiah frequently used thorns as a symbol for hardship and disaster—disaster that is a result of God's judgment. A powerful example is his description of the punishment God has in store for Edom: "Thorns shall grow over its strongholds, nettles and thistles in its fortresses" (Isa. 34:13). He seems to have chosen Edom as representative of the enemies of Israel, who attack "God's vineyard" in Isaiah 27, where the text also mentions "thorns and briers." Although the text in 27:4 is not clear, the meaning seems to be that the thorns are weapons of God against Israel's enemies. In the Isa. 7:23, "briers and thorns" represent the disaster that will befall King Ahaz and his people at the hands of the Assyrian king. The expensive, well-tended vines, "worth a thousand shekels of silver" (a shekel supposedly was about sixty cents), will be replaced by "briers and thorns" so hard and sharp they can pierce sandals, making people afraid to enter the fields. This was a fulfillment of the prophecy of disaster predicted in Isaiah's first Song of the Vineyard in chapter 5, when the vineyard "shall be overgrown with briers and thorns" (5:6). "Thorns and briers" appear again in chapter 32, as Isaiah describes the desolation that will fall on Judah with these words to the women harvesting the grapes:

> Beat your breasts for the pleasant fields,
> for the fruitful vine,
> for the soil of my people
> growing up in thorns and briers.
> (32:13)

Hosea, too, uses the invasiveness of thorns and nettles as a symbol of impending disaster at the hands of the Assyrians: "For even if they escape destruction, . . . nettles shall possess their precious things of silver; thorns shall be in their tents" (Hos. 9:6).

One of the most often quoted "thorn" phrases in scripture is Paul's "thorn in the flesh" (2 Cor. 12:7). We do not know whether this thorn was physical, mental, or spiritual, but it was more than just a nuisance. Paul obviously experienced it as something painful given him to keep him from being "too elated," or as biblical scholar Ernest Best says, "to save him from spiritual pride and, therefore, to advance the gospel."[1] Paul's first reaction, however, was a very human one: to pray for God to remove the thorn. Most of us, in times of physical pain or mental anguish, do the same thing. We beg God to take "the thorn" out of our lives. When Paul prayed in this way, he received an answer, but it was not the immediate removal of the thorn. Instead, he found comfort in Jesus' promise: "My grace is sufficient for you, for power is made perfect in weakness" (2 Cor. 12:9). Paul's "contentment" with the thorn was a recognition that even thorns have their purposes. Ralph Waldo Emerson expressed a similar idea, even using the word *pricked*, which suggests he had been reading Paul:

> Our strength grows out of our weakness. The indignation which arms itself with secret forces does not awaken until we are pricked and stung and sorely assailed. A great man is always willing to be little. Whilst he sits on the cushion of advantage he goes to sleep. When he is pushed, tormented, defeated, he has a chance to learn something; he has been put on his wits, on his manhood; he has gained facts; learns his ignorance; is cured of the insanity of conceit; has got moderation and real skill.[2]

Paul is saying something more in his letter to the Corinthians: that it is not just facts and skill we gain but a self-confidence based on a deep dependence on God. Our thorns are prickly reminders of our neediness and thereby keep us open to God's grace.

The Old Testament contains similar "thorny" references to trouble, pain, and aggravation: "thorns in your sides" (Num. 33:55) and "thorns in your eyes" (Josh. 23:13), for instance. Thorns and thistles as symbols of unwanted evil appear in such sayings as "Are grapes gathered from thorns, or figs from thistles?" (Matt. 7:16); "Thorns and snares are in the way of the perverse" (Prov. 22:5); "They have sown wheat and have reaped thorns" (Jer. 12:13).There is also the stern warning in Hebrews: garden soil that produces thorns and thistles "is worthless and on the verge of being cursed; its end is to be burned over" (Heb. 6:8).

There is great debate about the kind of thorns that composed the crown the Roman soldiers placed on Christ at his crucifixion. At least six types have been suggested, but the most frequently mentioned are Christ-Thorn and Spiny Burnet. This crown was not only an instrument of torture but the solders' derisive mockery of Jesus' claim to be a king. We can learn from Jesus' response to this treatment. Calvin commented that the amazing love exhibited in Jesus' willingness to accept such insults on our behalf should move us to "secret meditation, not fancy words."[3]

Jesus used the metaphor of thorns in his well-known parable of the sower to portray the way some people responded to his message. This is a parable about the difference between hearing and understanding. The seeds that fell among thorns represent those people who let the "cares of the world and the lure of wealth choke the word" (Matt. 13:22). Mark adds "and the desire for other things" (4:19), and Luke replaces that phrase with "pleasures of life" (8:14). We live in a time when many have heard the name of Christ, when the seed of the word has been widely sown. It is also a time accurately described by this parable, when willingness truly to "hear the word" and live by it has been choked out by all of these: the cares of the world, the lure of wealth, the desire for other things, and the pleasures of life. This growing indifference to Christian teachings that marks our century has caused analysts to call our age "post-Christian."

But in his commentary on Mark, Lamar Williamson says this parable

> speaks in both individual and corporate settings. It addresses the lives of persons who have heard the gospel but in whom it has not yet taken root; committed Christians who are for the moment spiritually dry; congregations, church boards, and whole Christian communions which are disheartened by periods of sterility. It speaks of a power whose life-giving potential is irrepressible.[4]

So this is a parable of optimism. It reminds us that in spite of indifference, opaqueness, distractions, spiritual dryness, the sterility or lack of growth of major denominations, the word of God will bear fruit, and the fruit will be beyond our expectations. It is a parable of encouragement to parents who grieve over their children's preoccupation with "the pleasures of life" and lack of interest in a living faith. It speaks words of hope to ministers and teachers who feel that the seeds they are sowing don't have a chance in the face of the choking thorns of the cares of the world and the lure of wealth.

It is also a parable with a question. It reminds us of the ups and downs of our own faith journeys; of our first enthusiasm, whose ardor faded with time; of how we allow demons of doubt and confusion to shake our faith; and above all, of the thorns in our lives that keep us from bearing fruit: stresses and worries and the insidiousness of greed, of always wanting "just a little bit more," of valuing a good time above spiritual growth and reflection. We succumb to the temptations of our age and culture and let thorns and thistles take over. The question the parable asks is about our openness to the words of the gospel. Will we receive these words with the receptivity of "good soil" and bear fruit, or will we let the good news be choked out by the "thorns" around us?

WEEDS: THE INCOMPREHENSIBLE PRESENCE OF EVIL

Darnel is perhaps the most well known weed in the scripture, although most of us know it as "tares" because of the line in the Thanksgiving hymn "Come, Ye Thankful People, Come": "wheat and tares together sown." The hymn refers to the parable of the weeds in the wheat in Matt. 13:24–30. The "weed" referred to has several names—bearded darnel, ryegrass, and tares—but its botanical name is *Lolium temulentum*. There are several fascinating things about darnel. First, it is extremely old; it has been found in four-thousand-year-old Egyptian tombs.[5] Second, it grows only among crops and damages them because of a poisonous fungus that lives in its grains. Third, it is almost indistinguishable from the wheat stalks among which it grows. As it develops, its roots entwine with the wheat roots, so that it is almost impossible to weed it out without pulling up the wheat. Fourth, it keeps its germination capacity for several years, so that in seasons of heavy rains it will spring up and completely overrun the wheat, which does not thrive in rain as the darnel does.[6]

At harvesttime, it was the custom for reapers to use sickles and cut both wheat and weeds together, separating them later. The weeds were tied into bundles to be used as fuel. The wheat was stored in underground pits lined with brick or in large pottery jars, not in "barns" as Matt. 13:30 states.

Matthew's parable of the wheat and the weeds is based on this harvest procedure. It contains some puzzling questions: If the slaves were farmworkers, wouldn't they know that wheat fields also produce weeds? And why did the landlord suspect "an enemy" of planting the weed seeds? Parables, however, are not always answerable to the processes of logic. They are told to make a point, in this case, what to do about the presence of evil in the Christian community. Our temptation is to root out evil when it surfaces in the form of heresy or unrighteous behavior, in order to preserve the integrity of the community. The problem is that we are not always correct about what constitutes either heresy or unrighteousness. But this parable suggests another solution, one that frees us from the dangers of our own zeal.

Last summer, I left my garden for a week during a time of heavy rain, and when I returned, I found that my pepper plants were nearly covered by grass, which had sprung up in a "demonic" way in the short time I had been absent. I tugged ferociously on those grass clumps to root them up but found that, in my fervor, I had pulled up not only grass but a pepper plant as well. It looked too much like the grass I was attacking.

The parable of the weeds and wheat is about this kind of misdirected zeal. What should be done about poisonous darnel that looks so much like wheat? The servants thought they knew; they asked for permission to uproot it. But the "householder" said no. He knew that the very act of pulling the weeds out might uproot the young wheat shoots, just as I uprooted my pepper plant when tugging on the grass around it.

This parable was addressed to the religious communities of Jesus' day—the Pharisees and the Qumran community, for example—who wanted a clear definition of "true believers." Jesus wanted to create a different kind of community: one that was not tightly defined, narrowly circumscribed. But doing away with borders and definitions and membership cards and "who's out and who's in" is frightening. The disciples were uneasy about this parable. They knew that getting rid of "weeds" makes us feel more secure as "wheat."

This is a parable also about humility and trust, patience and hope. It is a reminder that is not the responsibility of the servants to determine which are the poisonous plants and which are the good wheat. The sorting out will be done at the harvest by the Gardener who sowed the good seed in the first place. No matter how good our intentions are, we will most certainly, in our feverish ardor, pull up wheat instead of weeds.

The parable does not deny the existence of evil, both outside and inside the church. Instead, it suggests that the zealous may be going about preserving the "peace and purity" of the church in the wrong way. The movie *The Name of the Rose*, based on Umberto Eco's novel, graphically showed the horrors of the Inquisition in the fifteenth century. A woman was burned as a witch by the church in 1704 simply for wearing pants. The rack, the iron maiden, and the stake were not just instruments of war; they were tools of religious authorities who were determined to pull up the heretical weeds poisoning the true wheat of the body of Christ.

Today, many denominations are wrestling with issues on which faithful Christians are ardently divided. Are splits and schisms the necessary result of differing views on what scripture is saying about matters of faith? What alternatives does the "weeds and wheat" parable suggest? How can these alternatives be carried out with theological and biblical integrity? The parable raises serious questions, but it is crucial that the church wrestle with them if it is to continue to be the body of Christ in the world.

The function of the church is conversion and restoration of the sinful, in keeping with the mission of Christ, who came to call not righteous people but sinners to repentance. The very imperfection of the church proves its message: that good can overcome evil. In spite of the weeds, there will always be wheat. Calvin says,"The design of the parable is simply this: so long as the pilgrimage of the Church in this world continues, bad men and hypocrites will mingle in it with those who are good and upright." He adds that patience is necessary for our fight with evil, so that "in the midst of offenses which are fitted to disturb [us, we may learn to] preserve unbroken steadfastness of faith."[7]

The parable is a parable of grace. It reminds us to moderate our expectations about perfection. It asks us to recognize that only God is competent to decide where the weeds are in the church and to relinquish our feverish, arrogant efforts to eradicate them. But above all, it invites us to marvel at and celebrate the amount of good that exists in the church, in spite of its "weeds," because of God's grace.

As we think about weeds, it is important to remember that the gardens of our lives have them too. Our personal weeds may take any number of forms. Our crabgrass may be the need we have to "meddle," to hand out advice, to organize everybody around us. Our honeysuckle may be our need to cling to someone else for support and a sense of meaning; we can't disentangle from our children or spouses or even friends, so that their own growth is stunted as well as ours. Darnel may also grow in our gardens: our desire to persuade others we are better than we actually are. Or we may be plagued with temptations, which, like dock and dandelion, put down thick, deep-probing roots and come back year after year to infest our gardens. A gardening book warns, "Remember: *never trust weeds.* They have become very clever at survival over their long history, and one of their cleverest tricks is to look dead after you have dug them up, so that you do not bother to remove them. Never believe them. The tiniest dead-looking bit may contain enough life to start a new plant while your back is turned."[8] Evil operates in much the same way, as Paul knew: "For I do not do the good I want, but the evil I do not want is what I do" (Rom. 7:19). Its presence in the lives of the most devout Christians may be "incomprehensible," but it is nonetheless real and ready to spring to new life "when our back is turned."

PRUNING: GROWTH THROUGH DISCIPLINE

Pruning: it's so hard. Those graceful branches of forsythia and dogwood, of flowering peach and Judas tree, the flowering stalks of oregano and marjoram—

how can we bear to take shears to them? Yet gardeners know they have a responsibility to the plants in their care, a responsibility that includes the discipline of pruning. Pruning is necessary for shaping, for producing stronger growth, for getting rid of dead or diseased limbs. This process is a basic principle of horticulture. The cutting and trimming that seems so ruthless actually is invigorating and life producing. The result is more fruit, bigger blossoms.

The first mention of pruning in scripture is in Leviticus 25, where the rules about the sabbatical year for the land forbade pruning vineyards in the seventh year, the "year of complete rest" (Lev. 25:4). Pruning was necessary for a good grape harvest. The vines were planted in rows from eight to ten feet apart and were allowed to grow along the ground. After the vine budded and the clusters of grapes formed, the vines were propped up with sticks and the vinedresser pruned away the branches that had no fruit. This made the other branches stronger and their fruit bigger. Isaiah describes this process:

> For before the harvest, when the blossom is over
>> and the flower becomes a ripening grape,
> he will cut off the shoots with pruning hooks,
>> and the spreading branches he will hew away.
>> (Isa. 18:5)

The pruning hook was a simple tool—an iron blade attached to a handle. A blade of this type has been found, dating from 800 B.C.[9] Isaiah's description of the coming age of peace is symbolized not only by wild animals becoming a part of the fold (11:6–9) but by the often quoted passage about pruning hooks. It would not be at all impossible to reforge a spear into a pruning-hook blade.

> They shall beat their swords into plowshares,
>> and their spears into pruning hooks;
> nation shall not lift up sword against nation,
>> neither shall they learn war any more.
>> (Isa. 2:4)

Micah also quotes this poem but adds another line:

> But they shall all sit under their own vines and
>   under their own fig trees,
>   and no one shall make them afraid;
>   for the mouth of the LORD of hosts has spoken.
>   (Micah 4:4)

We long for such a peace-filled world, but we are also fearful of what it suggests. Is worldwide disarmament really safe? Will we ever be able to trust other people, other nations, enough not to be afraid? What if we turn our weapons into farming tools, and they don't? The answer is that the peaceable kingdom is possible only when all nations recognize the authority of God and are willing to live in obedience to it. When this happens, a society of men and women living together peaceably, without barriers of language, race, and class, will not be just an "impossible dream." Human lambs and calves will no longer have to fear human wolves and lions, but all will be a part of the same fold. In this passage we catch a glimpse of Isaiah's wonderful vision of God's sovereignty over all the earth, which is developed more fully in later chapters.

Pruning plays an important role in the famous "vine and branches" passage in John 15. Just as the vine was a symbol of Israel in the Old Testament (see Isa. 27:2–6), so it is used by John as a symbol for Jesus, the "true Israel" who completes and fulfills the mission of the old, "fruitless" Israel. Like all vines, this "true vine" has branches, and those branches are the followers of Jesus. Think how wonderful this image would have sounded to the disciples. It is a metaphor of intimacy, of closeness, of belonging. The branches "abide" in the vine; the disciples "abide" in Christ.

But there's a stern side in this metaphor as well, which the disciples may not have been as glad to hear. Like all vines, this one needs pruning. It is by careful pruning of the branches that a vine becomes fruitful. There is a play on words here, for the word for "pruning" is the same word for "being made clean" (*katharos*).

Pruning may be painful, but it is necessary that branches be "cleansed" of dead wood in order to grow. And so it is with Christ's followers.

The late Urban Holmes, dean of the Episcopal Seminary at Sewanee, Tennessee, understood this cleansing:

> Any good gardener knows that beautiful roses require careful pruning. Pieces of living plant have to die. It cannot just grow wild. We cannot simply "celebrate growth." It is more than to be regretted, it is tragic that we seem to have lost the insight that growth in Christ requires careful pruning. Pieces of us by our intentional action need to die if we are to become the person that is in God's vision. We are not cutting away a cancerous growth, but making room for intended growth.[10]

Are there pieces of our branches that need to be pruned? Galatians 5 contains a list of pruning that needs to be done if we are to produce the "fruits of the Spirit," in the form of "love, joy, peace, patience, kindness, generosity, faithfulness, gentleness, and self-control." Even if our "dead wood" is not licentiousness, sorcery, drunkenness, and carousing, most of us could stand some pruning of jealousy, anger, quarrels, dissensions, factions, and envy (Gal. 5:19–23). Pruning is an inward, continuous spiritual cleansing that enables us to carry on the work of Jesus in the world. It helps develop a strong connection between the vine and the branches, a connection necessary for faithfulness because, in the words of Jesus, "apart from me you can do nothing" (John 15:5). It is through that connection, through loving obedience to Christ, that we are able to bear much fruit and really become his disciples.

John says those branches that do not have this intimate relationship with Christ are cut away. The followers of Jesus stand under judgment, a judgment that is not harsh and vengeful but necessary so that richer, more abundant fruit will develop. An intimate relationship with Christ carries with its expectations—and demands. The expectation is that we bear fruit, bringing the good news of God's love to the world through our words and through our lives. The demand is that we "abide in Christ's love," so that his life-giving energy will flow through us and our joy will be complete.

A FINAL WORD

Weeds and thorns and thistles—not the most pleasant companions for gardeners. But even if "life is thorny," as Coleridge says, patient gardeners will learn that thorns have a purpose: they can be valuable reminders of our need to depend completely on the Master Gardener, whose Son also experienced the suffering thorns can cause. Confrontation with the thorns of life can be a means of grace.

Weeds teach us patience and humility. God knows a whole lot better than we do how to tell weeds from good wheat. And as symbols of our own imperfections, they remind us that the gardens of our lives cannot be weed-free unless we exert our energies to keep the weeds under control, so that the good seed of God's word will not be choked out but can grow and flourish and produce good fruit.

FOR SPIRITUAL GROWTH

1. We often speak of thorns in the flesh in a joking way. What have been your real "thorns in the flesh," the kind that made you realize your deep dependence on God? What are the thorns in the flesh in the life of the church?

2. Read Galatians 5:19–21. Jot down the areas mentioned in these verses where you may need pruning. If you have other "dead wood" that is not listed, write it down as well. Now create a prayer of confession, asking for God to prune all of this dead wood away.

3. Suggest that your congregation have a special church supper to honor the "saints of the church," both living and dead. Attach to a wall a long vine (either real or made from brown paper). Give everyone a branch-shaped piece of paper on which to write the name of a person from your congregation (or from the church at large) whose life has borne "much fruit." Attach purple "grape" circles on which to describe those fruits (examples:

"Faithfully delivered Meals on Wheels" or "Always ready to help"). At the end of the evening, read John 15:1–17, then read aloud the names and the fruits. Sing a hymn, such as "God Bless Your Church with Strength," by John A. Dalles (see *The Presbyterian Hymnal* [Louisville, Ky.: Westminster/John Knox Press, 1990]), or "For All the Saints Who from Their Labors Rest." Close with a litany of thanksgiving, using the names of the saints who have been described.

6   BRINGING IN THE SHEAVES

Hope and Thanksgiving

As long as the earth endures,
      seedtime and harvest, cold and heat,
summer and winter, day and night,
      shall not cease.
                              —Genesis 8:22

The harvest is plentiful, but the laborers are few;
therefore ask the Lord of the harvest
to send out laborers into his harvest.
                              —Matthew 9:37–38

So let us not grow weary in doing what is right,
for we will reap at harvest time,
if we do not give up.
                              —Galatians 6:9

Who loves a garden still his Eden keeps,
Perennial pleasures plants, and wholesome harvests reaps.
                              —Amos Bronson Alcott

Now God comes to thee,
not as in the dawning of the day,
not as in the bud of spring,
but as the sun at noon to illustrate all shadows,
as the sheaves in harvest, to fill all penuries,

all occasions invite his mercies,
and all times are his seasons.
                              —John Donne

Harvesttime! We long for it. It is the culmination of all our planning and preparing and waiting. The soil has been prepared by tilling and mulching; the seeds have been planted and watered. The warm sun calls the seeds to new life and abundant fruition. The result of our labor spills out of our gardens in a splendid cornucopia of red tomatoes, yellow squash, green cucumbers, purple eggplant, white cauliflower, and golden corn. Gardeners agree that there is no flavor as exquisite as that of tomatoes, corn, and peas fresh from the garden. The harvest season is the fulfillment of anticipation, of the hope that sustains us during days of toil.

BIBLICAL HARVESTS

In biblical times, harvests took place almost year round. Flax was harvested from March to April. The barley harvest came in April or early May, followed by the wheat harvest in May or June. In August and September, the summer fruits—figs, grapes, and pomegranates—were gathered, and the olives from September to November.

When biblical writers mention "harvesting," they are generally referring to the reaping of the two important grains: barley and wheat. When the wheat and barley were ready, the harvest had to be completed as quickly as possible. Everyone in the family helped. Proverbs 10:5 berates not only lazy adults but lazy children: the "child who sleeps in harvest" is shameful compared to the prudent child "who gathers in summer." Of course, the wealthy had servants, slaves, and hired laborers to bring in their harvests (see Matt. 13:24–30).

The gleaning laws decreed that fields were not to be stripped completely clean of grain and fallen grapes were to be left on the ground, so that poor people, widows, orphans, and strangers who possessed no land could find means of sustenance. Ruth's life was altered by this law, since she met Boaz, her future spouse, while gleaning barley in his fields (see Ruth 2).

Grain was harvested with a sickle, which cut off the stalks close to the ear. The grain was taken to the village threshing floor and usually threshed by the feet of animals or by sledges (see Isa. 41:15), which the children probably loved to ride. Winnowing—separating the grain from the useless chaff—was done by throwing the grain into the air with a fork so that the lighter particles (chaff) would blow away. It was this image that the psalmist had in mind when he compared the wicked to the "chaff that the wind drives away" (Ps. 1:4). After the winnowing, the grain was stored in pits, silos, cellars, granaries, and public storehouses.

The grape harvest began with laborers cutting bunches of grapes from the vine. The grapes were thrown into the wine press, which consisted of two pits hewn out of rocky ground. As the grapes were trampled by the feet of the laborers in one pit, the juice flowed into the other. This was a very noisy occasion, so much so that the roaring of God against the nations is compared to the loud shouts of "those who tread grapes" (Jer. 25:30). The juice was made into both wine and vinegar.

Harvesttime was a time of unrestrained joy. Isaiah uses the harvest to picture the joy the people will have under the coming messiah: "they rejoice before you as with joy at the harvest" (Isa. 9:3). The importance of this harvest joy in the lives of the people is vividly illustrated when Isaiah describes the grief and desolation of Moab in the wake of an invader in this way:

> The shout over your fruit harvest
>   and your grain harvest has ceased.
> Joy and gladness are taken away
>   from the fruitful field;
> and in the vineyards no songs are sung,
>   no shouts are raised;
> no treader treads out wine in the presses;
>   the vintage-shout is hushed.
> (Isa. 16:9–10)

HARVEST: A TIME OF THANKSGIVING

The people of Israel were full of anticipation as they settled into Canaan and planted their gardens, fields, and orchards. They looked forward eagerly to their first harvest. Would this land truly be a "land of milk and honey," the answer to their dreams?

God's promises to them had been quite explicit:

> For the LORD your God is bringing you into a good land, a land with flowing streams, with springs and underground waters welling up in valleys and hills, a land of wheat and barley, of vines and fig trees and pomegranates, a land of olive trees and honey, a land where you may eat bread without scarcity, where you will lack nothing, a land whose stones are iron and from whose hills you may mine copper. You shall eat your fill and bless the LORD your God for the good land that he has given you.
>
> (Deut. 8:7–10)

But God also gave them a rather stern warning: when they came into this land promised to them and had eaten their fill, they were to take care that they did not forget the God who had brought them out of Egypt, who had led them through the wilderness, fed them with manna and quail, provided water for them in the desert, and led them safely into this "good land" (Deut. 6:12).

The Israelites were eager to settle down, to exchange their nomadic lifestyle for an agricultural one. They were ready to work hard, to plow and plant and water. However, God saw the terrible temptation in all that industry: that their very self-sufficiency might cause them to forget to be grateful. We face that same temptation even more in our world today. How strange that we need to be reminded to be grateful when things go well for us, when our work is a success! How skimpy our prayers of thanksgiving are, compared to our prayers of desperation!

The three great annual pilgrim festivals—the Feast of Unleavened Bread, the Feast of Weeks, and the Feast of Booths—were "reminding times." They were explicitly designed for expressing gratitude to God for bountiful harvests and loving care, and to renew commitment to the one who had enabled them to "eat their fill."

The first of the festivals, the Feast of Unleavened Bread, probably began as a Canaanite agricultural feast and was adopted by the Israelites after they had settled in Canaan. It celebrated both the deliverance from Egypt and the beginning of the barley harvest, the first of the grains to ripen. The barley had been planted in the autumn, and now, with spring's arrival, the first of the harvest was ready to be gathered. A sheaf of barley, representing the early harvest, was offered to God (see Lev. 23:10). The new crop could be used for food after this official thanksgiving, but not before. This feast lasted for seven days, and about a week later, the wheat harvest began. The barley and wheat harvesting continued until the Feast of Weeks, fifty days after the offering of the barley sheaf.

The second festival, the Feast of Weeks, was the true harvest festival and is described that way in Ex. 23:16. This one-day festival got is name from the fact that it came at the end of the seven weeks of the grain harvest, which stretched from the first of the barley (usually in April) to the last of the wheat (sometime in May). It was a time of special sanctity, in which Israel recognized God as the source of rain and agricultural fertility. In describing Judah's faithlessness, Jeremiah refers to the Feast of Weeks: "They do not say in their hearts, 'Let us fear the LORD our God, who gives the rain in its season, the autumn rain and spring rain, and keeps for us the weeks appointed for the harvest'" (Jer. 5:24). This feast was also known as the "day of first fruits" (Num. 28:26), for it was the beginning of the season for voluntary offerings of the first fruits of the fields and gardens. As people brought these offerings, they uttered prayers of thanksgiving to God for their deliverance from Egypt and for the good land God had provided for them.

The Greeks called this festival Pentecost, since it came fifty days after the beginning of the barley harvest. It was a feast of solemn joy and thanksgiving for God's protection and care that had culminated in the successful harvest. The primary offering was two loaves of bread baked with the new wheat, presented by the priest on behalf of the people. Two lambs were also sacrificed. A fascinating element was the communal meal to celebrate "the bounty that . . . God has given." The poor, the stranger, and the Levites were invited to this meal, an act which recognized that gratitude to God is best expressed in sharing with others the good things God has provided (Deut. 26:11).

The third festival, the Feast of Booths, was celebrated in the autumn (usually October) after the entire harvest—not only grain but olives, grapes, and other crops as well—had been brought in. It was probably the original pilgrimage festival. The feast lasted for seven days, and every participant had to build a small "booth" to sleep in at night. The booths, constructed of branches and vines, were replicas of the small huts that people built in the fields and slept in to protect the olive orchards from thieves or wild animals. They were considered to be reminders of the time Israel spent in temporary shelters during the wilderness wanderings.

It was a happy occasion. There was a water-offering ceremony and a dance by the light of four huge menorahs (seven-branched candlesticks) that lasted most of the night. In Deuteronomy the people are told to "rejoice during your festival . . . for the LORD your God will bless you in all your produce and in all your undertakings, and you shall surely celebrate" (Deut. 16:14, 15); and rejoice they did. The Feast of Booths is a celebration of the equation: God's Blessing + Good Harvest = Great Joy.

The importance of these feasts is emphasized again and again in scripture. The Covenant Code, found in Ex. 20:22–23:33, reflects the life of the Israelites after their settlement in Canaan. One of the laws of this covenant was "You shall not delay to make offerings from the fullness of your harvest and from the outflow of your presses" (Ex. 22:29). In the renewal of the covenant after the second set of tablets was given to Moses, this law was spelled out even more explicitly: "You shall observe the festival of the first fruits of wheat harvest, and the festival of ingathering [Feast of Booths] at the turn of the year" (Ex. 34:22).

The Holiness Code of Leviticus, which interprets the meaning of holy living, included other laws about the harvest (Lev. 19:9; 23:22) which specified that some of the harvest of both grain and grapes must be left for "the poor and the alien." These gleaning laws reminded the people that just as God's holiness included generosity and grace to them, so must their holiness be defined by generosity and grace toward others. Deuteronomy reiterates the importance of this custom, adding widows and orphans to the poor and strangers (Deut. 24:19). Abundant harvests, the gift of God's grace, are to be shared.

HARVEST: SYMBOL OF JUDGMENT

Because being deprived of the harvest of grain and grapes was one of the worst calamities that could happen to the people of the Old Testament, crop failure naturally was a very powerful cultural and religious symbol of disaster. *Harvesttime* was seized upon by the prophets as a technical term to dramatize the judgment that would fall on the Gentile nations, who refused to acknowledge God, or even on God's people who no longer lived lives of covenant love and obedience and who abandoned God.

There were various warnings to the Gentiles:

1. In a warning to the residents of Damascus (capital of the Aramean kingdom to the north, threatened by the Assyrians), Isaiah predicts that the coming destruction will be as complete "as when reapers gather standing grain" and leave only a few pitiful gleanings (Isa. 17:5). In a later verse, he addresses their worship of "alien gods" by saying that the crops dedicated to them "will flee away in a day of grief and incurable pain" (Isa. 17:11).

2. Jeremiah uses various harvest images as symbols of the punishment awaiting Babylon, which had once been the dreaded enemy of Judah but which, in Jeremiah's time, was in danger from the Persians to the north. Jeremiah predicts that Babylon will be a besieged city, threatened with famine as both sowers and harvesters are cut off from it (Jer. 50:16). He adds that God will send "winnowers" to Babylon who will completely empty the land with their scythes of war, leaving behind only useless stubble (51:2). Babylon itself will be "harvested," but it will not be a time of rejoicing as the city will become "a perpetual waste." In another twist of the image, Jeremiah describes Babylon as a "threshing floor" waiting for the harvest of doom: "yet a little while and the time of her harvest will come" (51:33).

3. Joel compares the Gentiles to fields of ripe wheat ready for harvesting and to overflowing vats of grapes ready for treading when the day of the Lord comes (Joel 3:13). The book of Revelation uses a similar metaphor in 19:15. These verses are the source of the famous words in "The Battle Hymn of

the Republic," which also speak of God's coming judgment: "He is trampling down the vineyards where the grapes of wrath are stored."

4. Judgment was not for the Gentiles alone. Isaiah warns the complacent women of Judah, smugly satisfied about their good grape harvest, about the judgment that will come to them in the form of crop failure: "the vintage will fail, the fruit harvest will not come" (Isa. 32:10).

5. Hosea, too, sounds a warning to Judah of an appointed harvest of judgment (Hos. 6:11) if they do not return to God with "steadfast love and not sacrifice, the knowledge of God rather than burnt offerings" (Hos. 6:6). This chapter is one of the immeasurable pain and longing God feels for the beloved children whose devotion is not steadfast but evaporates as quickly as morning dew. The anguish of God is like the anguish of parents everywhere who ask their children: "What am I going to do with you?" (See Hos. 6:4.) Even though God longs to heal and restore the people, they continue to fail and, consequently, will bring the harvest of judgment upon themselves.

All of these messages of judgment begin to sound very depressing. We are like children who do not like to be scolded, even when we are wrong. So we turn to the New Testament for some relief from the prophets' stern reminders of the results of our disobedience, and what do we find? A fiery figure dressed in camel's hair and leather, shouting out a call to repentance exactly like those of the prophets! John the Baptist uses those same harvest-of-judgment images when he describes Jesus as the harvester who will "gather his wheat into the granary; but the chaff he will burn with unquenchable fire" (Matt. 3:12).

The parable of the weeds and the wheat in Matt. 13:24–30 is also about the harvest of judgment. The poisonous darnel, that insidious weed that looks so much like wheat, which will be sorted out by God, not us, will experience on the day of the harvest not only separation but judgment (Matt. 13:24–30). This judgment is pictured graphically in Revelation 14, as the Son of man wields his sickles to cut the "harvest of the earth" and "the clusters of the vine of the earth." In this passage, God's judgment is severe and prolonged, as "blood flowed from the wine press, as high as a horse's bridle, for a distance of about two hundred miles" (Rev. 14:20). The severity of this judgment is real, but it must be understood as the act of that loving and anguished parent of whom Hosea spoke, who has made every effort to bring the good news of salvation to "every nation and tribe and language and people" (Rev. 14:6).

It is important to remember that the central element in God's judgment is not hate but love. The longing of God in Hosea's writings, the passion and pain God feels for a wayward people that we find in Isaiah, Jeremiah, Micah, and Joel, are reminders that our God is a God who cares. God cares about the way we live, the kind of people we are. God cares about what we do to one another, and to ourselves. This God who loves us calls us out of our selfishness to "do justice, and to love kindness, and to walk humbly with your God" (Micah 6:8). And if we do not do these things, God says sorrowfully, we will harvest the fruit of our selfish disobedience and not the fruit of righteousness. The word *judgment* is related to the words *justice* and *righteousness*. Judgment is that part of the righteousness of God which calls us to lives of righteousness. It is the justice that gives meaning to the word *love*.

THE HARVEST OF RIGHTEOUSNESS

Paul used the metaphor of the harvest in a number of ways. First, at the close of his letter to the Galatians, he, too, speaks of the coming judgment in harvest language, as he tries to show the relationship of the future judgment to the present ethical behavior. His phrase "you reap whatever you sow" (Gal. 6:7) has become a familiar slogan, used by politicians as well as preachers. It has been called "the law of the identical harvest." If you sow corn, you harvest corn, not potatoes. If you plant thistles, you will reap thistles. Every gardener knows the reality of this.

Spiritual gardening works the same way. Anger, jealousy, and enmity breed more anger, jealousy, and enmity, in the same way that "murder shall breed murder," as George Bernard Shaw said.[1] The same thing happens with love. A friend whose husband grew up as a neglected child reflected, "He never learned how to love." The result was that he was unable to articulate his love for her, and the marriage died. When parents do not express love to their children, they sow seeds that will produce more lovelessness.

It is when we learn to plant the seeds of the fruit of the Spirit—"love, joy, peace, patience, kindness, generosity, faithfulness, gentleness, and self-control" (Gal. 5: 22)—and nourish them into maturity that we will reap eternal life, a life that begins now but that will have its full fruition at "harvesttime." In a similar vein, James says there will be a "harvest of righteousness" for peacemakers who sow the seeds of peace (James 3:18). This is the mirror image of Isaiah's words of hope "The effect of righteousness will be peace, and the result of righteousness, quietness and trust forever" (Isa. 32:17). Righteousness brings peace; peace brings righteousness.

Second, in Philippians, Paul also uses the term *harvest of righteousness* when he refers to "the day of Christ" at the end of the age. He expresses his hope that by that day the Philippians will have produced "a harvest of righteousness" that will result in "pure and blameless" lives (Phil. 1:11). He is careful to add, however, that this harvest of righteousness is not accomplished by sheer effort and determination but comes through faith in Jesus Christ. Righteousness is always the gift of grace.

Third, Paul expresses the same idea when he speaks of his own ministry and says that it is God who gave the growth (1 Cor. 3:6). This humility about ministry is hard to come by. We hate to let go the "ownership" of our work. "He is a member of *my* congregation," a pastor says proudly of someone with stature in the community. A youth worker claims about a young college graduate, "She was one of *my* young people!" We behave as if all the credit should go to us for the spiritual growth and maturity of those whom we teach. Those of us who have dedicated ourselves to developing garden plots of ministry for the kingdom find it especially hard not to feel that the plants growing in them are "ours." Some years ago, I left a job I had created and developed to enter seminary. It was very difficult for me to let go that garden plot which I had planted and cultivated. It was even harder when I became aware that certain of my favorite plants were dying because the new gardener was neglecting to give them proper nourishment, and that other seeds I had dreamed of planting still languished in their packets. I had to learn that Paul was right when he said, "Neither the one who plants nor the one who waters is anything, but only God who gives the growth" (1 Cor. 3:7).

Fourth, Paul gives the harvest of righteousness still another twist when he uses the term to encourage the church at Corinth to give more generously to the church at Jerusalem. He reminds the Corinthians that "the one who sows sparingly will also reap sparingly, and the one who sows bountifully will also reap bountifully" (2 Cor. 9:6). Then he suggests that just as God the Gardener provides seed and causes that seed to produce a harvest that will result in bread, so God will supply the seeds of generosity to produce a harvest of righteousness that will enrich the lives of the givers (2 Cor. 9:10). Paul seems to be speaking not only of spiritual blessing but of material blessing as well, an idea common in the Old Testament. He paraphrases Prov. 22:9, "Those who are generous are blessed," as "God loves a cheerful giver" (2 Cor. 9:7). In his commentary on 2 Corinthians, New Testament scholar Ernest Best suggests that Paul is so anxious to help the poor of Jerusalem that he doesn't hesitate to bring into play the self-interest of the Corinthians by promising them the reward of additional blessings.[2] However, the motivation of the giver is important: generosity is to be cheerful, not reluctant, forced, or calculating. The word *cheerful* in Greek is literally translated as "hilarious," and the phrase calls to mind the joyfulness that accompanied the grape and grain harvests. The harvest of righteousness is not a glum exercise of duty but a gleeful outpouring of joyful love and gratitude that results in blessings, for both the one who receives and the one who gives.

HARVEST: THE MISSION OF THE CHURCH

Jesus spoke of harvesting in quite a different way. As he looked about him at the "harassed and helpless" crowds (Matt. 9:36) he used words that sounded like those of the prophet Joel, who said, "The harvest is ripe" (Joel 3:14). But although the words are similar, there is a dramatic difference in meaning between the two sayings. Jesus is not calling down the wrath of God on sinful Gentiles, as the prophet did in Joel 3:13. Instead, he is challenging his followers to help him in his ministry of compassion. In Matthew, he is about to send the twelve disciples on their first mission, and in Luke, he is speaking to the seventy who were sent out in pairs. However, the task of ministry needs more than just seventy people. In both instances,

Jesus tells them to "ask the Lord of the harvest to send out laborers into his harvest" (Matt. 9:37–38; Luke 10:2). In John, Jesus uses these words of urgency in addressing the disciples after his conversation with the Samaritan woman at Jacob's well (4:35). In this passage, John is suggesting that the disciples are to harvest the fruit of the labors of Jesus. Paul understood his missionary work among the Romans as reaping a harvest (Rom. 1:13), one not of judgment but of salvation—a "gathering in" by "announcing the gospel of his Son" (Rom. 1:9).

Through the centuries, these passages have provided motivation for the missionary outreach of the church. Emil Brunner wrote, "The Church exists by mission, just as a fire exists by burning. When there is no mission, there is no Church; and where there is neither Church nor mission, there is no faith."[3] Brunner reflects the urgency of both Jesus and Paul, the urgency that caused the good news to become a flame spreading from Jerusalem to "Judea and Samaria, and to the ends of the earth" (Acts 1:8).

HARVEST OF HOPE

Balancing the image of the harvest of judgment is that of the harvest of hope. The parables of the sower (Mark 4:3–8) and the seed growing secretly (Mark 4:26–29) are parables of assurance. In telling them, Jesus, like the prophets, spoke of the coming of God's kingdom as a harvesttime, but this time it is a harvest of good news, of hope.

The parable of the sower, with its magnificent harvest yield of "thirty and sixty and a hundredfold" from the good soil, is a reminder that the kingdom will be abundantly above all that we can ask or think. It is an encouragement to remember that in spite of the frustrations and seeming futility of our labors in the kingdom, the harvest will come, and it will be beyond our imaginings. As biblical scholar Lamar Williamson says, "It speaks of a power whose life-giving potential is irrepressible."[4] We are to be faithful sowers of the seed of the word and to remember that it is God who brings the growth.

The parable of the grain growing secretly takes this thought even further. We are to be faithful as the farmer is faithful, who plants and waters and fertilizes, yet still is amazed by the miracle of growth, by the wheat that springs from tiny grains, by the grapes that hang lusciously from the vines. It's as if the earth itself produces these crops and the farmer has almost nothing to do with it. Every gardener with any sense of humility at all has experienced the same feeling. Even though we may boast about what kind of organic fertilizing we've done or how we produce our compost, we are still conscious of the miracle that takes place quite apart from our efforts. Last year I planted three small pineapple sage plants. To my complete amazement, they sprang up into bushes six feet high, covered with lovely, sweet-smelling red flowers much loved by yellow butterflies. Those bushes were a complete serendipity, a gift, a miracle.

So it is with the kingdom of God. The harvest is sure. We are to be faithful in our effort but still remember who the real Gardener is. Rachel Henderlite, professor of Christian education at the Presbyterian School of Christian Education and Austin Seminary, liked to remind her students, "Never think you are going to go out and bring in the kingdom." We plant and water, and when it is time, it is God who brings the day of "gathering in," the time of harvest, a time of both judgment and joy. All that is necessary is to take God seriously.

HARVEST HOME: FULFILLMENT OF ANTICIPATION

The wonderful old phrase "harvest home" is not used much in our technological age. But in agrarian societies it had three meanings. First, it meant the end of the harvest season, when all the crops are "brought home" for winter storage. Shakespeare had this meaning in mind when he compared a certain lord's newly shaved chin to a "stubble-land at harvest-home" (*King Henry IV*, Part I). The second meaning was a festival, like the Feast of Booths, celebrating the final ingathering of the harvest with joy and thankfulness. The third was a harvest song, sung by the workers as they brought in the very last load of the harvest. Henry Alford used this meaning in his popular Thanksgiving hymn "Come, ye thankful people, come, raise the song of harvest home."

This was a time for which the farmers waited in eagerness and longing. This waiting for harvest home became a beloved metaphor for the anticipation of the coming of the messiah in the Old Testament and of Christ's return at the end of the age in the New Testament. James describes this eager anticipation in this way:

> Be patient, therefore, beloved, until the coming of the Lord. The farmer waits for the precious crop from the earth, being patient with it until it receives the early and the late rains. You also must be patient. Strengthen your hearts, for the coming of the Lord is near.

> (James 5:7)

Harvest home is coming! the prophets cried, and the finality of that coming is heard in their messages of both judgment and hope. There will be a good harvest on the day of the Lord for those who return to God with steadfast love and repentance, but there will be crop failure for those who do not.

Psalm 126 is almost certainly a "harvest home" song. It speaks of those who "come home with shouts of joy, carrying their sheaves" (Ps. 126:6). It was probably sung as travelers went up to Jerusalem for one of the harvest festivals. The psalm celebrates both past and future: it is a song of thanksgiving for God's deliverance and a prayer for a reversal of fortune (which might refer to the crops of the coming year) that will bring joy to lips and tongues. If sung at the harvest festival, it was also a song of thanksgiving for the harvest completed and safely home. Some scholars think that this psalm refers to the end of the age, when God will change the course of the people's fortunes and they will celebrate with a harvest-home song of joy. Psalm 126 is a psalm of consolation and hope. It reminds us that whatever our distress, whatever our sorrow, the God that has done great things for us in the past will see us through new difficulties to a glorious harvest home, and we will be joyful once again.

In Isaiah, there is a suggestion of a harvest-home festival in the banquet that will take place when the messiah comes, when the Lord will make for all people "a feast of rich food, a feast of well-aged wines, of rich food filled with marrow, of well-aged wines strained clear," and at which God "will wipe away the tears from all faces" (Isa. 25:6, 8). A later passage contains a more complete description of the joyful fulfillment of the harvest home to come:

> For I am about to create new heavens
>   and a new earth;
> the former things shall not be remembered
>   or come to mind.
> . . . .
> They shall build houses and inhabit them;
>   they shall plant vineyards and eat their fruit.
> They shall not build and another inhabit;
>   they shall not plant and another eat;
> for like the days of a tree shall the days of my people be,
>   and my chosen shall long enjoy the work of their hands.
> (Isa. 65:17, 21–22)

This is the promise of a joyful harvest, of a garden that brings full satisfaction, of life lived in all the fullness of God's grace. This "new earth" will be a place not of idleness but of satisfying work that is not vain and pointless. True shalom will reign as it did in the original garden.

John quotes this passage when he describes the harvest that will take place in this new heaven and new earth, where God wipes away tears and death and mourning and pain (Rev. 21:4). The harvest comes not from fields of grain but from "the tree of life with its twelve kinds of fruit, producing its fruit each month; and the leaves of the tree are for the healing of the nations" (Rev. 22:2). C. S. Lewis, in his children's story *The Last Battle*, drew on this image from Revelation for his description of a place the children reach at the end of their adventures:

> At last . . . they saw a smooth green hill. Its sides were as steep as the sides of a pyramid and round the very top of it ran a green wall: but above the wall rose the branches of trees, whose leaves looked like silver and their fruit like gold.
>   "Further up and further in!" roared the Unicorn, and no one held back. . . .
> Only when they had reached the very top did they slow up; that was because they

found themselves facing great golden gates. And for a moment none of them was bold enough to try if the gates would open. They all felt just as they had felt about the fruit—"Dare we? Is it right? Can it be meant for *us*?"[5]

Can it be meant for *us*? A harvest home of life and healing, of freedom from pain and death. A harvest home that will be the fulfillment of everything we ever wanted, of all our dreams and anticipations. God's word answers with an emphatic "Yes!" The harvest home *is* for us.

And people will come from "east and west and north and south" to sit at that great Thanksgiving table—a table that is the ultimate gift of God: a harvest home of good things, a celebration of the bountiful love and overwhelming generosity of the Gardener who cares for us, sustains us, and gives us living water.

> The earth has yielded its increase;
>   God, our God, has blessed us.
> May God continue to bless us;
>   let all the ends of the earth revere him.
>   (Ps. 67:6–7)

A FINAL WORD

The metaphor of the garden teaches us many things. It teaches us that the Good Gardener has planted a garden for us to live in. It teaches us that we are stewards of that garden, to till and care for it and to do so with awareness, attentiveness, and appreciation. As we work the soil, as we water and weed it, as we carefully prune away dead wood, we learn from our tasks about our needs. We learn that we, too, must be friable soil that is receptive to God's word, that we need the water of life for our growth, that we must never turn our back on the weeds that infest our lives, that God's pruning makes us fruitful.

And finally, it teaches us about the joy of harvest home. In spite of our times of dryness and unproductivity, in spite of our thorns and weeds, the garden tells us there is hope. It teaches us that through our repentance and the steadfast love of the

Good Gardener, we can anticipate a harvest of righteousness instead of a harvest of judgment. The fruit of the tree of life is for us. For this we can truly "raise the song of harvest home."

FOR SPIRITUAL GROWTH

1. Make a list of the things for which you are most grateful in your life. Now write a prayer of thanksgiving and gratitude for this harvest.

2. Set aside an amount of money for each vegetable, fruit, flower that you harvest. Keep the tithe in a jar on your table and donate the money to a feeding program for the homeless. When you place your tithe in the jar, say this prayer:

   Creator God, we offer this tithe with gratitude for the many gifts you have given us. May the fruits of the soil and of our labors assist in nourishing those who have no place to plant. Bless them and all our companions on this earth.[6]

3. On a piece of paper, write down one other thing you (or your group) can do to alleviate world hunger. If you are in a group, share ideas and make a commitment to carry out at least one of the ideas.

4. Read or sing the hymn "Come, Ye Thankful People, Come." What scripture passages do you find reference to in this hymn?

NOTES

CHAPTER 1: GARDENING IN BIBLICAL TIMES

1. Michael Zohary, *Plants of the Bible* (Cambridge: Cambridge University Press, 1982), 21.
2. C. C. McCown, "Geography of Palestine," in *The Interpreter's Dictionary of the Bible* (Nashville: Abingdon Press, 1962), 3:636.
3. Zohary, *Plants of the Bible*, 21.
4. Oded Borowski, *Agriculture in Iron Age Israel* (Winona Lake, Ind.: Eisenbrauns, 1987), 87.
5. For the information about planting and harvesting, I am indebted to both Borowski, *Agriculture*, 57–69, and Madeleine S. Miller and J. Lane Miller, *Harper's Encyclopedia of Bible Life*, 3d ed. (San Francisco: Harper & Row, 1978), 174–79.
6. Zohary, *Plants of the Bible*, 56.
7. A. W. Anderson, *Plants of the Bible* (London: Crosby, Lockwood & Sons, 1956), 9.
8. Ibid., 9.

CHAPTER 2: THE GARDEN OF THE LORD

1. Walter Brueggemann, *Genesis*, Interpretation: A Bible Commentary for Teaching and Preaching (Atlanta: John Knox Press, 1982), 40.
2. John T. McNeill, ed., *Calvin: Institutes of the Christian Religion*, vol. 20 of The Library of Christian Classics (Philadelphia: Westminster Press, 1960), 199, 1.16.2.

3. Wayne Martindale and Jerry Root, eds., *The Quotable Lewis* (Wheaton, Ill.: Tyndale, 1989), 257.

4. Calvin, *Institutes,* 53, 1.5.1.

5. Walter Brueggemann, *First and Second Samuel*, Interpretation: A Bible Commentary for Teaching and Preaching (Louisville, Ky.: John Knox Press, 1990), 255.

6. Calvin, *Institutes*, 199, 1.16.2.

7. From *Prayers for Puppies, Aging Autos, & Sleepless Nights: God Listens to It All*, by Robert Jones (Louisville, Ky.: Westminster/John Knox Press, 1990). Used by permission of Westminster John Knox Press.

8. Edwina Gateley, *I Hear a Seed Growing* (Trabuco Canyon, Calif.: Source Books, 1990), 42.

9. Anne Frank, *The Diary of a Young Girl: The Definitive Edition* (New York: Doubleday, 1995), 196.

10. William Griffeth, ed. *The Garden Book of Verse,* (New York: William Morrow & Co., 1932), 6.

11. Sidney Lanier, "A Ballad of Trees and the Master," in *The Story of Jesus in the World's Literature,* ed. Edward Wagenknecht (New York: Creative Age Press, 1946), 175.

12. Eco-Justice Task Force, *Keeping and Healing the Creation* (Louisville, Ky.: Committee on Social Witness Policy, Presbyterian Church (U.S.A.), 1989), 46.

13. Beth Richardson, from *Alive Now* (Jan.–Feb. 1991), copyright ©1990 by The Upper Room. Used by permission.

CHAPTER 3: CONNECTING WITH CREATION

1. Geoffrey Norman, "MM Interview: Edward O. Wilson," *Modern Maturity* (May–June 1995), 63–67.

2. Shannon Jung, *We Are Home: A Spirituality of the Environment* (New York: Paulist Press, 1993), 60.

3. Jill Smolowe, "Intimate Strangers," in *Time,* special issue (spring 1995), 20–24.

4. John T. McNeill, ed., *Calvin: Institutes of the Christian Religion,* vol. 20 of The Library of Christian Classics (Philadelphia: Westminster Press, 1960), 199, 1.16.1.

5. Thomas Berry, *The Dream of the Earth* (Sierra Club Nature and Natural Philosophy Library; San Francisco: Sierra Club Books, 1988), 23.

6. Linda Filippi, quoted in Avis Crowe, "Gardening as Sacred Activism," *Radical Grace,* published by the Albuquerque Center for Contemplation and Action (Oct.–Nov. 1994): 8.

7. Wendell Berry, *The Unsettling of America: Culture and Agriculture* (New York: Avon/Sierra Club Books, 1977), 138.

8. Walter Brueggemann, *The Land* (Philadelphia: Fortress Press, 1977), 59.

9. Douglas John Hall, *The Steward: A Biblical Symbol Come of Age* (Library of Christian Stewardship; New York: Friendship Press, 1982), 111.

10. Sallie McFague, *Models of God: Theology for an Ecological, Nuclear Age* (Philadelphia: Fortress Press, 1987), 13.

11. From Vera K. White, *Healing and Defending God's Creation: Hands On! Practical Ideas for Congregations* (Louisville, Ky.: Office of Environmental Justice, Presbyterian Church (U.S.A.), 1991), Appendix 1.

12. Henlee Barnette, *The Church and the Ecological Crisis* (Grand Rapids: Wm. B. Eerdmans Publishing Co., 1972), 81.

13. Douglas John Hall, *Imaging God: Dominion as Stewardship* (Grand Rapids: Wm. B. Eerdmans Publishing Co., 1986), 204.

14. This idea and the one above have been adapted from White, *Healing and Defending God's Creation.*

CHAPTER 4: LIKE A WATERED GARDEN

1. Simon Cohen, "The Negeb," *The Interpreter's Dictionary of the Bible* (Nashville: Abingdon Press, 1962), 3:532.

2. Quoted in *With All God's People: The New Ecumenical Prayer Cycle. Orders of Service,* compiled by John Carden (Geneva: World Council of Churches Publications, 1989), 64.

3. In *Enfolded in Love: Daily Readings with Julian of Norwich* (Minneapolis: Seabury Press, 1981), 20.

4. Richard Foster, *Prayer: Finding the Heart's True Home* (San Francisco: Harper-Collins, 1992), 17, 24.

5. Raymond Brown, *The Gospel according to John (i–xii),* Anchor Bible (Garden City, N.Y.: Doubleday & Co., 1966), 178–79.

6. Carolyn Huffman, *Meditations on a Rose Garden* (Nashville: Dimensions for Living, 1995), 28.

7. From Vera K. White, *Healing and Defending God's Creation: Hands On! Practical Ideas for Congregations* (Louisville, Ky.: Office of Environmental Justice, Presbyterian Church (U.S.A.), 1991).

Notes

CHAPTER 5: WEEDING AND PRUNING

1. Ernest Best, *Second Corinthians*, Interpretation: A Bible Commentary for Teaching and Preaching (Atlanta: John Knox Press, 1987), 119.
2. In *The Complete Essays and Other Writings of Ralph Waldo Emerson*, ed. and with a biographical introduction by Brooks Atkinson (New York: Modern Library, 1950), 184.
3. John Calvin, *A Harmony of the Gospels Matthew, Mark and Luke*, trans. A. W. Morrison, Calvin's Commentaries, ed. David W. Torrance and Thomas F. Torrance (Grand Rapids: Wm. B. Eerdmans Publishing Co., 1972), 3:189.
4. Lamar Williamson, *Mark*, Interpretation: A Bible Commentary for Teaching and Preaching (Louisville, Ky.: Westminster John Knox Press, 1993), 91.
5. Michael Zohary, *Plants of the Bible* (Cambridge: Cambridge University Press, 1982), 161.
6. "Weeds," *Fauna and Flora of the Bible* (London: United Bible Societies, 1972), 194–95.
7. John Calvin, *Commentary on a Harmony of the Evangelists* (Grand Rapids: Baker Book House, 1979), 2:119.
8. Alec Bristow, *The Easy Garden* (New York: Thomas Y. Crowell, 1977), 119.
9. Paul Garber, "Pruning Hooks," in *The Interpreter's Dictionary of the Bible* (Nashville: Abingdon Press, 1962), 3:941.
10. Urban T. Holmes, quoted in Carolyn Huffman, *Meditations on a Rose Garden* (Nashville: Dimensions for Living, 1995), 45.

CHAPTER 6: BRINGING IN THE SHEAVES

1. George Bernard Shaw, *Caesar and Cleopatra*, act IV, in *Four Plays by Bernard Shaw* (New York: Modern Library, 1953), 185.
2. Ernest Best, *Second Corinthians*, Interpretation: A Bible Commentary for Teaching and Preaching (Atlanta: John Knox Press, 1987), 86.
3. Emil Brunner, *The Word and the World* (London: SCM Press, 1931), 108.
4. Lamar Williamson, *Mark*, Interpretation: A Bible Commentary for Teaching and Preaching (Atlanta: John Knox Press, 1983), 91.
5. C. S. Lewis, *The Last Battle* (London: Bodley Head, 1956), 176.
6. Beth Richardson, from *Alive Now* (Jan.–Feb. 1991), copyright © 1990 by The Upper Room. Used by permission.